A Funny Way of Being Serious

James A Simpson

Savage
LONDON AND EDINBURGH

Steve Savage Publishers Ltd
The Old Truman Brewery
91 Brick Lane
LONDON
E1 6QL

www.savagepublishers.com

First published in Great Britain by Steve Savage Publishers Ltd 2005
Reprinted 2009

Copyright © James A. Simpson 2005

ISBN: 978-1-904246-17-6

Typeset by Steve Savage Publishers Ltd
Printed and bound by the Cromwell Press Group

Contents

Prologue

Dr James Simpson is one of Scotland's treasures and one of the Kirk's treasures. Long before I could lay claim to the enriching experience of his personal friendship, I had admired and respected his insights into Christian belief and the prodigious fund of wisdom and humour in his many books.

When over forty years ago I played Prospero at Stratford, an unsympathetic critic likened my portrayal to an incarnation of the rather dour Scottish philosopher Thomas Carlyle. Perhaps the said critic was unaware of one of Carlyle's less well-known utterances, his claim that true humour sprang more from the heart than the head, that its essence is love, not contempt. How precious is the gift of kindly humour, the ability to laugh at ourselves and at incongruous happenings. When I arrived at John Brown's shipyard to commentate for the BBC on the launch of the *QE2*, one shipyard worker approached me. 'Excuse me,' he said, 'I don't want to insult you, but are you Tom Fleming?'

My reaction on reading Dr Simpson's latest anthology could best be described in a line from my well-known fellow actor, Will Shakespeare: 'I did laugh sans intermission...' My sheer delight was heightened by the knowledge that the royalties from this book will hopefully bring to a magnificent total of £50,000 the money raised over the years by Jim for research into Cystic Fibrosis. This is a cause especially dear to him, for it could yet bring blessing and benefit to the future of countless young people, including his own beloved grand-daughter Sally. I commend these pages to you most warmly – even at the risk of your knowing whence I stole all my best jokes!

Tom Fleming

Introduction

Charles Dodgson, who chose the pen name Lewis Carroll, tells how he wrote his 'nonsense' stories for the children he loved, 'not for money and not for fame, but in the hope of supplying some thoughts that may suit those hours of innocent merriment which are the very life of Childhood; and also in the hope of suggesting to them, and to others, some thoughts that may prove not wholly out of harmony with the graver cadences of life.'

My aim is similar, to provide adult readers not just with stories that will hopefully bring a smile to their faces, but also with stories which will cause them to stop and reflect on some of the more serious aspects of life. Believing that the human mind resembles a picture gallery more than a debating chamber, I have over the years sought to develop and embellish the art of illustration, and story-telling. What power a good story has to inform, delight, enlighten, and hammer home a point. Humour is a kind of court-jester in the castle of our souls, by which we are protected from too solemn a view of our own importance, and are sometimes led to say, 'God be merciful to me a fool.' I feel sorry for those who lack a sense of humour, those who seem not to have a funny bone in their body. This book is a blend of seriousness and affectionate fun, of sense and nonsense, for though kindly laughter is precious, it is not by itself a sufficient resource to satisfy our deeper hungers, or help us cope with life's many incongruities and jumbled contradictions.

Though story-telling and humour lose something when written, the writer having none of the props available to the teacher, comedian and after-dinner speaker – the modulated voice, the accented adjective, the facial expression, the hand movements, the calculated pause, the change in pace – yet I have been encouraged by the fact that readers of my previous books have thanked me for bringing the saving and redemptive sense of humour into their lives and giving them food for thought. I hope this book will do the same. When the American humorist Mark Twain died, Henry Van Dyke said of him, 'He did not laugh at the weak, the helpless, the true, the innocent; only at the false, the pretentious, the vain and the hypocritical.' I would accept that for my own epitaph. Throughout the pages of this book I have studiously avoided humour that is offensive or vulgar. I often wonder what those who are gratuitously

7

offensive are trying to prove. Though their rude and crude jokes and bawdy stories may get cheap laughs, they seldom enlighten or make people feel better about themselves and the world.

Jane Austen once said, 'People are more ready to borrow and praise my books, than buy them.' I hope that will not be true of this book, for once again it has been written to raise funds for a very worthy cause. All the royalties go to Cystic Fibrosis Research, a debilitating disease from which many children suffer, including my oldest and much-loved grand-daughter Sally.

My sincere thanks are due to my wife Helen, Professor Peter Howie and Muriel Armstrong for reading the manuscript and making helpful suggestions, also to Tom Fleming, the distinguished Scottish actor and broadcaster, for readily agreeing to write the foreword, and to my publisher Steve Savage.

James A. Simpson

A Funny Way of Being Serious

We cannot live by seriousness alone. I doubt if I could have survived in the ministry for more than forty years, if I had not had a sense of humour, the ability to laugh at my own foibles and pretensions, and to laugh a little bit more quietly at other people's foibles and pretensions. Many in positions of authority, and those who aspire to occupy such positions, those who have a 'career' to carve, and a 'big impression' to make on the world, sometimes make the monumental blunder of thinking they must look frightfully serious in order to keep themselves in the saddle. The protruding jaw, determined chin and pouched lower lip replace the warm smile. The ability to laugh at ourselves is the best antidote I know for all forms of pomposity, sham, academic nonsense and social humbug.

❋

Laughter is a healing elixir of great power. Dr Adams, a physician in Washington DC, pointed out how getting a suicidal person to laugh can often be a turning point. 'Many a suicidal call to my office has begun with the words, "Doctor I want to kill myself."' On receiving such a call he would ask, 'At your place or mine?' When, as often happened, the caller would laugh, Dr Adams would invite them over to talk. Humour is part of the human survival kit. It is good medicine. In *Tom Sawyer* Mark Twain writes of the old man who 'laughed joyously and loud, shook up the details of the anatomy from head to foot, saying that such a laugh was money in a man's pocket because it cut down the doctor's bills.'

❋

Whereas wise-cracking is simply playing with words, wit at its finest has truth in it. It is significant that the words wise and wit come from the same root. Here we have a reminder that wit can convey wisdom. The wise man and the wit, the sage and the jester are twins — not identical twins, but twins nonetheless. The problem with many who have trouble swallowing the Book of Jonah, is that they fail to realise that this humorous fishy story, written by a minor Jewish prophet, has a major serious message. This whale of a tale was written to try and get the racial and religious exclusivists of the third century BC to face up to certain uncomfortable home truths about themselves.

✳

When Mr Schulz, the inspiration behind the Peanuts cartoon series, died, a fellow-cartoonist depicted Schulz and Snoopy arriving at the pearly gates. Though on the gates there was a large notice which read, 'No Dogs ALLOWED', St Peter says to Mr Schulz, 'I think in this case we can make an exception.' Behind the cartoon humour associated with Snoopy and his friends there was often the still small voice of social commentary. That is also true of the rollicking mirthquake of *The Simpsons*. How often that animated TV series is a funny way of being serious.

✳

Few people are more aware of the disarming and reforming power of humour than the Scottish columnist Ron Ferguson, the former leader of the Iona Community. In his book *The Reluctant Reformation of Clarence McGonigall*, Ron uses a larger-than-life central character to highlight some of the absurdities of ecclesiastical life, and to poke fun at a small minority in the church who have a ladder to climb, and a great impression to make. The year is 2009AD. The centralisation of ecclesiastical power in the hands of a few, the church's new marketing slogan, 'Smile with Jesus', the proposal that communion services be sponsored by Hovis bread, and ministers be paid by results, greatly upsets the Rev Clarence McGonigall, a cantankerous but insightful churchman, who is about to retire. Reluctant to accept the church's relentless attempts to be 'with it', involving mobile phones, bonding sessions and the latest computer technology, Clarence often froths at the mouse! Ron's book, which is a delightful blend of seriousness and humour, is a welcome change from the many earnest and largely inconsequential volumes about church reforms which have been produced in the last decade. Ron justifiably believes it might even have a greater impact, that through the mirthquake the still small reforming voice might just be heard.

✳

Many of the most successful situation comedies on television have been a funny way of being serious. In a tribute to Ronnie Barker, Sir Peter Hall said, 'Comedy has to be serious and true to life.' Though the characters in most sit-coms are always slightly larger than life, the people portrayed in them have their counterparts in everyday life. I think of Victor Meldrew in *One Foot in the Grave*, the spokesman for 60-year-olds who have been thrown on the scrapheap, and for those who are certain that the good old days were so much better than the present. In every community there are such grumpy old men with very limited patience. There are also, in most suburban areas, women like Hyacinth in *Keeping up Appearances*, with their aristocratic dreams and Jean Brodie vowels. There are also dubious characters like Del Boy in *Only Fools and Horses*, ever the optimist. Having once heard a pessimist defined as someone who lives and works with a perpetual optimist, is it really surprising that Rodney has so many low days? When the situation comedy *Till Death Us Do Part* was first screened, there existed people like Alf Garnett, who had a rabid paranoia about coloured people and how Britain was declining. Far from being an attempt to brutalise people of other races, that programme was an attempt to poke fun at the Alf Garnetts of this world with their half formed opinions and deep rooted prejudices. The writer Johnny Speight said, 'I did not create Alf Garnett. Society created him. I am simply reporting him." The string-vested TV character Rab C. Nesbitt provided greater insight into underclass domestic life in Britain in the 1980s than many well-meaning, but humourless documentaries. Comedy is a serious business.

❋

G. K. Chesterton wrote, 'Angels can fly because they take themselves lightly. Solemnity flows out of people naturally; but laughter is a leap.' I wish more of us made that leap. Too often we forget that we are most ridiculous when we take ourselves too seriously. Not every business, family or personal problem is a matter of life and death. David Jason recently expressed his regret that unlike the pubs in *Only Fools and Horses*, which are a great source of wit and much laughter, the pubs in the popular soap *EastEnders* have little or no humour. It is all so deadly serious. The clients seem to have forgotten that kindly laughter and a smiling face can brighten life and lighten many an ordeal — whether that of lying in a hospital bed, or waiting for hours in a traffic jam, or facing the burden of grief.

❋

Our ablest cartoonists and comedians highlight some of the absurdities and idiosyncrasies of our so-called civilised life. Humour has a critical role to play in sweeping the world free of shams, superstitions, outworn customs and false beliefs, in exposing human imperfections and wilful distortions. 'You gotta say this about the white race,' said one comedian, 'its self-confidence knows no bounds. Who else could go to a small island in the Pacific, where there is no poverty, no crime, no unemployment, no war and few worries, and call it a primitive society?'

The cartoon on the front cover depicts two farmers fighting over a cow, one pulling at its head, the other at its tail. Down below are two lawyers milking it! That picture is worth a thousand words. How often the only people to benefit from bitter disputes are the lawyers. I also love the mild irony of the reporter who said, 'The best acting at Academy Awards ceremonies is done by the losers congratulating the winners.'

Time and time again the light infantry of humour achieves more than the heavy artillery of harsh criticism. To highlight the absurdity of the infighting that sometimes occurs within religious institutions over what are relatively trivial issues, the 'straining at gnats and the swallowing of camels', the Chief Rabbi Jonathan Sacks told a story about a Jew called Cohen who shortly after moving home attended the local synagogue, one which did not have a resident rabbi. The welcome was warm. The singing was good. Each Sabbath all went fine until it came to the reading from the Torah. Then pandemonium broke out. Half of the congregation stood and shouted to the others, 'Ignoramuses. You must stand when the Torah is read.' But the others shouted back, 'Heretics. You must sit when the Torah is read.' Week after week the same thing happened. Finally Cohen consulted an aged, learned rabbi in a neighbouring city. 'Tell me, Rabbi. When the Torah is read in synagogue, should we stand?' The Rabbi stroked his beard and said, 'No that is not the tradition.' 'In that case, should we sit during the reading of the Torah?' 'No,' says the Rabbi, 'That is not the tradition.' 'Rabbi,' said Cohen, 'The reason I ask is that in my synagogue, half the congregation stand and half sit, and they start shouting at each other.' On hearing this the Rabbi nodded, 'Yes, that is the tradition.'

Such timely humour can often bring people to their senses and get them moving towards an acceptable compromise or solution. St Basil could have strongly criticised those in the early Church who wanted to run off into the desert and lead a hermit life. But instead, recalling Jesus' instruction to his followers 'to wash one another's feet', he said with a spice of humour, 'If you always live alone, whose feet will you wash?'

❃

In similar vein, instead of saying, 'Be wary of investing in the stock market,' Mark Twain said, 'October is one of those peculiarly dangerous months to speculate in stocks. The others are July, September, April, November, May, March, June, December, August, January and February!'

❃

As a raconteur the bulky brilliant Peter Ustinov was unsurpassed. His sparkling *bon mots* and agile wit captivated his hearers. Whereas many might have said of the filming of *Spartacus*, in which Ustinov played a leading role, that it took an interminable time to make, he said, 'It wasn't an assignment. It was a career... It took longer to make than the event it was about... My youngest daughter, Andrea, was born when I started filming. By the time I'd finished she was asking my wife where I'd been.' Ustinov made many a penetrating social comment in jest. 'Beware of experts. The day humans blow up the world with the Bomb, the last survivor will be an expert saying it can never happen.'

❃

In our day most bookstores have shelf-loads of self-help books which tell the reader how to achieve happiness, career advancement, find the right soulmate, overcome depression and put the magic back into a marriage. Recently as I dipped into a few of these 'feel-good handbooks' I began to feel anything but good. I began to wonder whether the strong feelings I had had for 45 years, that my marriage had been a good one, and that my working life had been very satisfying, were all in fact an illusion.

How could I possibly have been happy when I did not regularly read books about improving sexual satisfaction, or repeat several times each day such positive mantras as 'I believe in me' or 'Every day in every way I am getting better and better', which I obviously am not?

How could I possibly experience personal fulfilment

• when I did not make time to do regular breathing or yoga exercises, or attend Tai Chi classes

• when I had not written my own personal reflective journal, or enjoyed candlelit baths

• or when I had not smiled at the sparkling diamond droplets flying through the air as a passing car completely soaked me as I walked for the morning paper?

❋

In the introduction to his autobiography, Ronnie Corbett makes a serious point about life's unpredictability in a delightfully humorous way. 'If I had known when I was young that I was going one day to write my autobiography, I would have lived my life differently. I would have organised my career into chapters, and I would have met my friends in alphabetical order – to help with the index. The dramas and the cliff-hangers would have been spaced out evenly. Unfortunately it has not been as tidy as that... Events occurred at inconvenient times.'

❋

Many a truthful word is spoken in jest. Bob Dole quotes two comments of President Reagan: 'One way to make sure crime does not pay would be to let the government run it... Government does not solve problems; it either subsidises them or rearranges them.'

❋

The London subway on which I was travelling was so packed that when, at the next station, even more people came on board, an attractive young woman, in an attempt to ease the congestion, put her newly purchased plastic pail over her head. As she did so, a stranger standing nearby said, 'Lassie, you are not that bad looking.' The ensuing laughter eased the tension. The person who said, 'If you don't have a sense of humour, you probably don't have any sense at all', was overstating the case, but there is no doubt that when we lose our sense of humour, we begin to lose not only perspective, but our footing.

Self-Deprecating Humour

'He is not laughed at who laughs at himself first.' Thomas Fuller

Self-deprecating humour is always delightful, whether it be Jimmy Durante poking fun at his nose or Ronnie Corbett at his diminutive stature, or Dawn French at her considerable girth, or Victor Borge at his piano playing, or Victor Mature at his acting ability. When Victor Mature was turned down for membership of an exclusive American country club because he was an actor, the self-effacing Victor replied, 'I'm no actor, and I have got 64 films to prove it.'

✳

Addressing a group of students in 1962, Senator Robert Kennedy said, 'You exemplify what my brother meant when he said in his inaugural presidential address, "Ask what you can do for..." *No that is not right...* "Do not ask what you can do..." *That is not right either...* "Ask not what you can do for your country but..." *Well anyway, you remember his words.'* Robert Kennedy concluded his embarrassment by saying, 'That's why my brother is President and not me.'

✳

A radio announcer recalled how he had a phobia about the pronunciation of the name of the distinguished Russian composer Rimsky-Korsakov, who wrote so many wonderful tunes including *The Flight of the Bumble Bee.* The announcer had difficulty enough pronouncing the surname, let alone Rimsky-Korsakov's Christian names – Nikolai Andreievich. On one occasion he heaved a sigh of relief after pronouncing the surname correctly, but then proceeded to say, 'Let us listen now to *The Bum of the Humble Flea.'*

✳

A friend tells how his first and last attempt to shine in a university debating competition fell at the first fence. 'After I had spoken, the adjudicator remarked that I looked like the best speaker until I had actually spoken.'

✳

Talking of past successes and failures, Peter Ustinov told how his second play, *Blow Your Own Trumpet,* was well and truly lacerated by the press, but not the public. 'They,' he said, 'were not there.'

Tom Fleming is so well endowed in voice and pitch, that he could thrill an audience even by reading a financial report. When Tom is not leading worship in his home church, he is usually playing the organ. He regularly pokes fun at his organ-playing ability, which in fact is very good. He tells how one Sunday during his opening voluntary, one of the office-bearers came and placed a Havana cigar in his top pocket. At the end of the service, as the people were leaving to Tom's accompaniment, the same office-bearer came and removed the cigar, saying, 'You were not worth it!' Tom also relates how a squirrel once ran round the window ledges outside the church, before settling on the ledge behind the organ. After the service several worshippers informed him how during his playing, the squirrel had sat seemingly entranced by the music. 'No,' said another worshipper. 'It had its paws over its ears.'

＊

A woman recalls receiving an award at the annual company dinner. As she was returning from the stage, she tripped, dropping the trophy on the chairman's toe. As she bent to pick up the broken prize, she ripped her skirt. Recalling this unflattering story, she said, 'None of this would have been so bad if it had not been an award for managing the department with the best safety record.'

＊

Humour-coated self-criticism can be very appealing. A speaker at a dinner told how he was such a plain looking child, that the first time he played Hide and Seek, no one came looking for him. That endeared him to his audience.

＊

In the introduction to his book, *Frankly Speaking*, Frank Sellar tells a lovely story against himself. While on holiday near Port Stewart in Northern Ireland, he and his wife decided to try and learn to play golf. They had several lessons from the local professional before venturing out on the course. There being a crowd of people waiting to begin their round, they fell into conversation with a Belfast man and his ten-year-old son. The father invited them to join them in playing the nine-hole course. Both father and son were good players. Towards the end of the round when the Belfast man asked Frank what his job was, Frank replied, 'What do you think I do?' The man having suggested a doctor or a teacher, Frank said, 'No, I am a clergyman.' 'Och,' said the Belfast man, 'I should have guessed. Only a minister could play as badly and not swear.'

✳

A golfer whose dream was one day to break a hundred would sometimes counter the amazing feats of the other golfers in the monthly medal by telling how at one hole he actually had a six-foot putt for a par, and at two of the others, if he had sunk his chip, he could have got a birdie!

> *Some golfers lie awake at night*
> *And brood on what went wrong;*
> *I'd rather think of what went right –*
> *It does not take so long.*

President Ford, who was an incredibly erratic golfer, once told how he waited until he had hit his first drive before deciding which course to play. With tongue in cheek, Bob Hope compared his own golfing ability to the golfing prowess of Arnold Palmer. 'Palmer has won as much money as I have spent on golf lessons!'

✳

Gene Perret, one of Bob Hope's finest scriptwriters, told how when his little daughter was asked to recite a poem of her choice at kindergarten, he offered to write a poem for her. But she declined: 'No Dad, this is in front of the whole school. I want it to be good.'

✳

The actress Rosalind Russell recalled how one day, on the deck of a luxury liner, she was sitting next to a man with a terrible cold. She suggested he go to bed early, drink a lot of fluids and take two aspirins. She told him he would feel a lot better in the morning. He smiled but made no verbal response. So she said, 'My name is Rosalind Russell. You know I make movies.' The man thanked her and said, 'My name is Charles Mayo, and I run a medical clinic.' She had given free medical advice to one of America's most distinguished doctors.

✳

The Victorian journalist G. K. Chesterton was a man not only of ample girth, but ample mirth. When the First World War broke out, a broken right arm that had not been set properly disqualified him from the infantry. The fact that no horse could carry his colossal bulk, over 300 lbs, put the cavalry out of the question. To the recruiting officer he finally said, 'Could I not even form part of a barricade?' When, a few months later, an indignant aristocratic English lady asked him, 'Why are you not out at the front?' he coolly replied, 'Madam, if you will step round this way a little, you will see that I am.' No one laughed louder at his own jokes than Chesterton, but as they were usually at his own expense, that did not spoil them. He once suggested that he was one of the most generous men in Britain. 'When I rise in a crowded bus, I make it possible for two old folk to be seated!'

❋

A Glasgow man was heard to mutter as he slung yet another betting slip in the bin, 'My luck is such that if I bought a cemetery, folk would stop dying.'

❋

Presidential candidate Adlai Stevenson often used self-deprecating humour. He loved to tell of a Democratic Convention at which he was the main speaker. Right at the front of the hall was an attractive but very pregnant Stevenson supporter. She was carrying a plaque proclaiming 'Adlai's the man'.

❋

An actress had been so impressed by the flattering series of photographs taken by a particular photographer, that ten years later, even though he was retired, she pleaded with him to take her picture again. When shown the proofs she said, 'Oh dear, you make me look so much older than last time.' With great tact the photographer replied, 'Ah yes, but I was younger in these days.'

❋

When Al Purdy was introduced on a radio programme as one of Canada's finest poets, he told the interviewer she would be nearer the truth if she described him as a 'high school dropout, a bankrupt businessman, an inconsiderate son, a problem husband and a demoted soldier'. In fact, he said, he had been demoted so often while in the armed forces, he had finally found himself saluting civilians!

✳

Many reckon George Bush's best speech was the one he delivered to the Gridiron Club. For more than a hundred years, the club has gathered together Washington's media and political elite. That night the President endeared himself to his audience with self-deprecating humour. He struck back at those who regularly suggest he is not very bright intellectually, that he is lazy, inarticulate, not up to the job, that it is in fact Vice-President Cheney who makes all the important decisions. That night Bush told his audience, 'To those people who say... ' Then he stopped, and casting a deadpan nod in the direction of Cheney, said, 'Dick, what do I say?' The audience roared with laughter. Then the President continued, 'These stories about my intellectual capacity do get under my skin. You know for a while I even thought my staff believed them, for there on the schedule first thing every morning it said, *Intelligence Briefing*... I hope those who have mapped the human genome might make it possible to clone another Dick Cheney. Then I won't have to do anything.' That night he also admitted to suffering foot-in-mouth disease. He even quoted Garrison Keillor: 'George Bush's lips are where words go to die.' Some commentators believed this self-deprecating speech was proof that the President has a better ear for wit than many of his detractors imagine he has. That could be. On the other hand it could be that there are some very clever and humorous script writers in the White House!

Names and Nicknames

Names are important. It is by our name that we are introduced and remembered. In one sense our name is our humanity. One of the most chilling aspects of the German concentration camps was that once people entered, they became numbers. They lost the identification by which they were known to the world. To strip people of their names is almost as degrading as stripping them physically naked. Recall Jesus' significant question to the tormented man who kept pigs in the territory of the Gaderenes: 'What is your name?' To his fellow Gadarenes he was a man without a name — at best a poor soul — at worst a social menace banished to the caves. But for Jesus, knowing the man's name was important.

❋

A four-year-old who had finished at nursery school had been told that after the summer holidays, he would be going to the big school. 'You won't have any naps during the day,' said his mother, 'and you'll have a new school-bag with books and a pencil case.' The wee lad, having pondered all this, asked, 'Will my name still be Alec?'

❋

When Stravinsky was fifty-eight he applied for American citizenship. At his first interview the official asked the famous composer his name. 'Stra-vin-sky,' he replied, speaking each syllable clearly. 'You could change it, you know,' suggested the official. Stravinsky declined. With the exception of a few who seek stardom, such as Camille Javal, who changed her name to Brigitte Bardot, or Charles Buchinsky, who changed his surname to Bronson, most of us carry the same name throughout our entire life.

❋

The name by which a child is known can so affect a child's self-image and perception, that there is now a scholarly discipline devoted to the study of names — ONOMASTICS. In one of his stories, P. G. Wodehouse has Bertie Wooster, the vacuous man-about-town, and Jeeves, his ever-resourceful valet, discuss a mutual acquaintance. 'Is his name Lemuel?' said Bertie. 'I fear so, Sir,' said Jeeves. 'Could he not use his second name?' 'His second name is Gengulphus,' said Jeeves. 'My goodness Jeeves,' said Bertie, 'There is some raw work pulled at the font from time to time, is there not?'

The Puritans often engaged in such raw work! They gave their children names such as *Valiant for Truth, Precious Promises, Patience* and *Higher Ground.* Names can still be the cause of acute teenage embarrassment. I wonder if in years to come, embarrassment will cause David Beckham's son Romeo to change his name. When Cruz, the third Beckham child was born, his oldest brother having been called Brooklyn after the New York district where he was conceived, a cartoonist posed the question, 'Do you think Cruz was conceived on the *QE2?*'

✻

A teacher tells how he had a Jacqueline Hyde in one of his Perth classes. Her parents had obviously not thought of their chosen name's similarity to the infamous Jekyll and Hyde. In my wife's class there were twins, Chrysanthemum and Delphinium. They quickly became known as Chrissie and Delphi. It obviously never occurred to the parents of Fortune Borthwick what would result when 'Miss' was put in front of their daughter's name. When she left home she used her middle name!

✻

Many men call their sons after them, but fortunately few do what the boxer George Foreman did, named all four of his sons George. In the Highlands a hundred years ago it was customary even for daughters to be called after their father or grandfather. Numerous were the Georginas, Williaminas, Jamesinas. When Nigel Lawson the former chancellor of the Exchequer called his daughter Nigella, it occurred to me that it was just as well Salman Rushdie did not follow the same practice or his daughter would have been called Salmanella!

✻

Tom Wharton was for many years one of Scotland's most distinguished soccer referees. Mr Wharton, who was six feet four inches tall, was known as *Tiny* Wharton. Tom laid great stress on formality. In addressing the players there was no Dick or Harry. It was Mr X or Mr Y. He expected the same respect in return. His commanding presence was a crucial advantage on the pitch. Players often looked ridiculous as they sought to argue the toss with him. One classic confrontation was with Johnny Hamilton of Hearts FC. Now there was not a malicious bone in Hamilton's body, but he did often confuse the functions of an outside left with those of a counsel for the defence. In football circles his affectionate nickname was *Yapper*. On the pitch his voice was often thick and indistinct, for he had lost most of his teeth on various football grounds throughout the country. He always left his dentures in the dressing room before the match started.

On the day of the classic confrontation Mr Hamilton, early on in the game, had voiced his disapproval of several of Mr Wharton's decisions. Believing that it was the duty of a referee, if at all possible, to keep 22 players on the field, Mr Wharton gave him several chances to repent of his verbal indiscretions. But finally he had to caution him with a yellow card. Unfortunately within a few minutes Johnny overstepped the mark again. For a brief moment the two men were outlined against the sky rather like the *Queen Mary* and a small fussy tug. Slowly Mr Wharton reached for his note-book. 'Mr Hamilton, I have to take action against you for persistent dissent. You have already been cautioned, but apparently without effect. I am therefore ordering you from the field.' He cut magisterially through Hamilton's attempted protests. Knowing how often Mr Hamilton spoke and joked about his majestic dentures, he wound up the proceedings by saying with good-humoured steel in his voice. 'Mr Hamilton, the time has come for you to rejoin your teeth.' Johnny had the grace to laugh.

✳

Elphinstone Dalglish, a former assistant chief constable for Strathclyde Region, was a member of my Glasgow congregation. One morning as he was driving in the rush hour along Great Western Road, one of the main arterial routes into the city, he got stuck behind a car parked outside a newsagent shop, even though numerous signs clearly stated that parking was not permitted between 8 and 9.30AM. Trying to edge out past the parked car he accidentally grazed the side of it. At that moment the owner came out of the shop. Having drawn in beyond the parked car, Mr Dalglish suggested that before exchanging insurance details, they should both drive round the corner out of the main stream of traffic. 'No, no, I have met your kind before,' said the man, cursing and swearing like a trooper, 'once you get into that car, I will never see you again.' The man was apparently still fuming when he arrived at his office. There he told a colleague how a stupid driver with an equally stupid name like Elphinstone Dalglish had dented his new car. Apparently he turned ashen grey when his workmate informed him that that was the name of the assistant chief constable!

During his sermon on the text from Ezekiel, 'No reward is given unto you', a visiting priest to a church in Dundee said several times, 'I desire no reward.' The smiles on the faces of some of the worshippers puzzled him. What the priest did not know was that the lady organist's name was 'Nora Ward'.

✳

A few ministers in Scotland still farm the church glebe land. Some keep sheep, others sow potatoes and turnips. A few years ago at a Perth farm auction, one such minister put in a successful bid for an old tractor. The auctioneer, who is renowned for his ability to remember names and faces, said to the purchaser as he sounded his gavel, 'I feel I should know your name.' 'Yes,' said the purchaser, 'you probably should. I am your minister!'

✳

At a Perthshire luncheon I was seated next to a Hazel Barbour, a lovely lady in her 70s. What a delightful dinner companion she was. On enquiring about her family, she told me she had only intended to have four, but her fourth pregnancy had resulted in twin girls. There being no ultrasonic scans in these days, she had not known until the moment of birth that she was having twins. Shortly after being admitted to the hospital in the early stages of labour, she had a lengthy chat with the nursing sister on duty. 'What are you going to call the baby?' the sister asked. 'If it is a girl,' said Hazel, 'we are going to call her *Kate*.' The following day, just after Kate was duly born, the doctor informed her there was another baby. A few minutes later what Hazel initially thought was an identical twin sister was born. Returning with the second baby duly bathed, the sister asked, 'And what are you going to call this one?' Hesitating just for a moment, Hazel said, 'I think *Duplicate*.'

✳

A maternity nurse tells of another patient who had undergone a Caesarean section. When after the operation the nurse handed the mother her baby, she informed her she had a healthy baby boy. Still groggy from the anaesthetic, the new mother asked, 'What is his name?'

A Ronnie Clubb from Peterhead told me how, prior to his marriage, in order to acquire passports for his fiancée and himself, he had sent off the necessary forms and photographs, duly attested by the minister who was to perform the ceremony. Weeks passed without result. Finally he phoned the passport office. The following day he received everything back, with an accompanying note: 'Error in application'. He scrutinised the forms but could see nothing wrong, until he checked the names on the back of the photographs. On the back of his photo the minister had written, 'I hereby certify that this is a true likeness of the Rev William H. Brown', and on his fiancée's, 'I hereby certify this is my wife Mrs Brown.'

✳

When Terry Venables was manager of Crystal Palace Football Club, he had on his books two players, one called Jim Philip and the other William Queen. In the course of a match which Crystal Palace was losing, some of the players started accusing their own team-mates of not giving 100% in effort. Eventually a fight broke out between two of the Crystal Palace players, Jim Philip and William Queen. When the local reporter sent in his match report, the sub-editor of the London *Evening Standard* gave it a heading which captured the attention of many London readers: '*Philip and Queen in Palace Brawl*'.

✳

Shortly after moving to Dornoch I was invited to take part in the annual man-boy golf competition. The day before the tournament, my son informed me that I was playing with 'Onion'. Protesting that I could not walk on to the first tee and say, 'Hello, Onion,' I asked what his real name was. 'Dad, I don't know. Everyone just calls him "Onion", but if it is any help he is a close friend of "Cabbage".' I was soon to discover that almost every pupil had a nickname. Because our youngest son Alistair lived in the manse, he quickly became known as Alimanse. There were so many Frasers, Cummings and Mackays in the neighbouring village of Embo that the old council records of house-owners included the nickname, or by-name as it was often called.

✳

Three names dominate the Ladies Championship notice-board in the Royal Dornoch Clubhouse – a Mrs McCulloch, a Mrs Booker-Milburn and a Mrs Mackay. For twenty years scarcely another name appears. What many visitors do not realise is that Mrs McCulloch, Mrs Booker-Milburn and Mrs Mackay were the same lady.

❋

In the world of golf there have been some delightfully appropriate surnames — a Mr Hooker and a Mr Slicer, a Mr Putt and a Mr Wood. In the Bing Crosby tournament, among the invited guests one year was the Episcopal Bishop of Los Angeles — the Rev William Swing. At least these names are easier to spell than that of the former Open champion, Mark Calcavecchia.

❋

The former European Ryder Cup Captain, Sam Torrance, tells of playing once with the American professional Jesse Snead. The subject of their conversation turned at one point to dogs. Both were the proud owners of Labradors. 'Strangely enough,' said Jesse, 'my labrador is called Sam.' Sam smiled and said, 'That *is* strange. Mine is called Jessie.'

❋

An American friend who owned a small printing business tells how May and June were his busiest months. Then he had to work closely with the editors of school magazines, and meet strict deadlines. One year after the publication of one such magazine, a teacher came and complained about the nickname printed under his picture. His complaint was not the inclusion of the other teachers' nicknames, but the inclusion of his — 'Big Ears'. He felt that any reputable printer would have censored the printing of such a nickname. I don't know what it was about that story, but I began to find myself paying far more attention to people's ears. I discovered that just as no two people have the same fingerprints, so no two people have identical ears. Some have ears with a twist in them, others have cabbage ears, some have very red ears, some have big lobes and others small lobes, some have ears that lie flat against their heads, others that stick out at right angles. Observing people's ears gradually became an addiction with me. It threw faces out of all proportion. It spoiled many a lovely face. All I saw were people's ears. It was rather like studying one of those puzzle pictures. To begin with you cannot see what you are told to look for, but once it is pointed out, you can see almost nothing else. How guilty many of us are of doing something similar, if not with people's ears, with their skin colour, ethnic origin, religious affiliation, or political leanings.

The first time I visited the United States I travelled on board the *Queen Mary*. I recently learned that Cunard had originally intended to name the liner *Queen Victoria*. This would have been in keeping with the names of previous liners like the *Lusitania*, and *Aquitania*, all of which ended in the letters '*ia*'. But one evening over dinner, in response to a question from King George V concerning what they were going to call their new liner, the Cunard director told the King they were thinking of naming her after Britain's finest Queen. 'Oh,' said King George V, 'Mary will be thrilled.' To save royal embarrassment they named her *Queen Mary*!

✳

A man with a goatee beard works for the Highland Region environmental health department. One of his responsibilities is to collect 'wheelie bins' laden with garbage. He is such a kindly man that he does not deserve the nickname he has acquired, 'Wheelie Bin Laden'.

✳

On display in the fraud department in the FBI building in Washington are examples of fraudulent cheques used by one forger. He obviously had a twisted sense of humour for he always signed the cheques U. R. Sunk, or I. A. M. Fraud

✳

There are questions concerning names to which there seems to be no uniform answer.

Why do some people prefer to be an FIP person – a first initial person – J. Paul Getty, F. Scott Fitzgerald, J. Edgar Hoover?

Why do others prefer to be a one name person – Madonna, Liberace, Cher?

Why do yet others prefer three names – Robert Louis Stevenson, Charles Rennie Mackintosh, George Bernard Shaw, Andrew Lloyd Webber?

I am sure psychologists could have a field day.

Heart Problems

'The heart's aye the part aye, that makes us right or wrang.' Robert Burns

Of one man it was said that he never had a bad word to say about anyone – the reason being that he always spoke and thought about himself. Aldous Huxley wrote about such people. The titles of his novels are significant – *Brief Candles, Barren Leaves.* Self-centredness and self-pleasing can lead to all kinds of heart problems. The philosopher Descartes got it wrong when he said, 'I think therefore I am.' Much nearer the truth is 'I love, therefore I am.' Shakespeare also got it wrong when he wrote, 'To be or not to be, that is the question.' 'To care or not to care', that is the question. If we don't have caring love in our heart, we have the worst type of heart trouble.

❋

The best exercise for the heart is to reach down and lift someone up. We were made to serve one another, not just ourselves. We are not here solely for our own happiness.

> *There is a destiny that makes us brothers,*
> *None goes his way alone.*
> *All we send into the lives of others*
> *Comes back into our own.*   (Edwin Markham)

To restore an old house is exciting. To restore joy in a lonely heart is more exciting still. Life is enlarged and enriched when we seek another human being in need of a little time or friendliness or help, or some worthwhile cause that needs a little support.

❋

When the American psychologist William James was a boy, he wrote to a friend about a summer house in New Hampshire which his family had acquired. He was very excited about it. It was a wonderful house. All the doors opened outward. What a great way to live, the doors of the mind and heart opening outward.

❋

The offer of Norbert Reinhart, aged 49, a Canadian mining company owner, to swap places with one of his employees who had been taken hostage by rebels in Colombia, touched many Canadians. Reinhart was 94 days in captivity before being released. The employee Edward Leonard (aged sixty) had just been with the firm for a week. When released, Reinhart seemed stunned to find that he had become a kind of national hero. *The Montreal Gazette* wrote, 'In an era when employees often feel their bosses really don't care about them, the gesture captured the popular imagination.'

❋

A friend who tried hard at dinner parties to be friendly, entertaining and amusing, finally realised that the secret of being a good dinner guest is to say to those seated next to you, 'Tell me more about what you do. It sounds fascinating.' In similar vein a professor told his students, 'The world doesn't want to see your sore toe. It wants to show you its sore toe.'

❋

The Italian priest Father Borelli once spoke in Falkirk about his work in Naples with the *scugnizzi* – the street urchins. He told how he had finally obtained permission from the archbishop to take off his clerical clothes and dress as a *scugnizzo* and live with the boys in their appalling environment, and thus try and improve their lot – which he did. The loveliness of Father Borelli's character, his inner joy and serenity, made an unfailing appeal to all who heard him that night, as it had done several weeks before to a national audience, when he had appeared on the popular TV programme *This is Your Life*. Father Borelli's closing remark to his audience was, 'The poorest person is the one who is incapable of sharing his personality, incapable of loving.' Sitting next to me that night was a successful company director. On the way home he said that any degrees, any wealth he had, he would gladly exchange to be as compassionate and inwardly content as Father Borelli. Many that night realised that money and fame are not the way to measure success and self-worth

❋

We dislike selfishness and envy, but see them every day in the mirror. Shakespeare's words about Cassius apply to many. 'Such men as he be never at heart's ease, while they behold a greater than themselves.' The distinguished American Dr Henry Ward Beecher had great difficulty in accepting the fame and acclaim that his sister Harriet Beecher Stowe received when her book *Uncle Tom's Cabin* appeared. He was certain there was only room for one distinguished person in the Beecher family. Mozart, one of the greatest natural geniuses music has produced, was fiercely jealous of the pianist Clementi, whom some regarded as an even finer pianist. Fifty years ago Bertrand Russell, the philosopher and mathematician, was almost as famous as anyone in the English-speaking world, yet a close friend tells how Russell was upset because he was not as well known or highly regarded as Albert Einstein.

❋

For one year, my wife and I lived in a house in Charlotte Square in Edinburgh which had formerly been the home of the outstanding Scottish preacher, Dr Alexander Whyte. Dr Whyte once had as his assistant a Hugh Black, who was later to become the professor of preaching in Union Seminary in New York. One of the church members jokingly said that whereas Dr Whyte blackballed the saints, Hugh Black whitewashed the sinners. As the years passed, Hugh, who had caught the ear of the younger generation, began drawing even larger congregations. Whyte once confided to a friend what problems that caused him. The friend, knowing what a saintly person Dr Whyte was, and how absolutely loyal to his assistant, said he had difficulty believing that. 'Ah,' said Dr Whyte, 'you don't know the black depths of the human heart.' Alexander Whyte was more honest than most.

❋

All of us have to deal with four types of people—

Those less prosperous, less able and less influential

Those with whom we have many things in common, but whom we surpass in a few things

Those who have certain things in common with us, but in other things just surpass us

Those who far excel us

In our dealings with the first two groups, those whom we surpass, envy does not enter the picture. Nor does it enter with the fourth group. Students are seldom envious of their professors. Most golfers are not really jealous of Tiger Woods or Ernie Els. Such immense golfing ability awakens aspiration, not envy. They so

29

surpass us that no real comparison is possible. We are also not in active competition with them. It is the third group, those who have been running alongside us, but suddenly forge that little bit ahead, that constitute the critical moral problem — those who pip us at the post, who get the promotion we want, or win the game we wanted to win, who marry the person we wanted to marry, who become more popular or prosperous than us, who can afford designer clothes and exotic holidays, whose family at school get better grades. Most people understand what Shakespeare was getting at when he wrote,

> *The General's disdained*
> *By him one step below,*
> *He by the next,*
> *That next by him beneath;*
> *So every step.*

It is not so much that we are prejudiced against others; the problem is we are born prejudiced in favour of ourselves. The human heart finds it more difficult to rejoice with those who rejoice than to weep with those who weep. Is it not significant that though we have words like compassion and sympathy to describe sharing another's pain, we lack words meaning to rejoice in another's joy? So devilish can envy be on occasions that we cannot hear of the advancement, success, or luck of a friend without a pang of envy. We have difficulty accepting that others should have some advantage over us. This is illustrated in the story of an Englishwoman, a Frenchman and a Russian who are each given a single wish by one of those genies whose almost relentless habit is to pop out of bottles. The Englishwoman says that a friend of hers has a charming cottage in the Cotswolds and that she would like a similar cottage with the addition of two extra bedrooms, a second bathroom and a river running past the back garden. The Frenchman says his best friend has a gorgeous blonde wife. He would also like a blonde wife but with longer legs and a bit more in the way of culture and *chic*. The Russian, when asked what he would like, tells of a neighbour who has a cow that yields a vast quantity of the richest milk, which in turn yields the thickest cream and purest butter. "I vant dat cow," the Russian tells the genie, "dead."

Once envy takes root, rational thought can quickly wither and die. With what loathing envy often eyes a more courageous or capable person. With what backbiting and sneers it can express itself. Who ever heard people pass scrupulously fair judgments about those who surpass them, or those who surpass their children. Mozart described Clementi's compositions as worthless, and his piano playing as having 'not a farthing's worth of feeling'. To what terrible lengths envy can drive people. Recall Tonia Harding the American skating star, who arranged for a hitman to cripple her rival for Olympic gold.

✳

The story is told of a competitor in the early Olympics who refused to accept that taking part was more important than winning. He was so jealous of the man who beat him into first place in the marathon that, under cover of darkness, he chiselled away at the base of the statue which had been erected in honour of the winner. When the statue toppled, it fell on him and killed him. How often envy has consumed the person who envies.

✳

Envy chills life at the centre. It is a cancer which, if allowed to enter the soul, harms the mental and spiritual health of the victim. It being too ugly a feeling to admit to others, we make such an effort to camouflage it that we usually end up disguising it from ourselves. The Italian painter Giotto depicts envy with large distended ears, a creature eager to hear anything bad about a worthier neighbour. Envy being so closely linked with greed, Giotto portrays envy as clutching a bag of gold in one hand and reaching out with the other, his fingers sharpened to claws. Envy also being very cunning Giotto pictures a serpent springing from the mouth of envy. But there is still more to envy, and Giotto knew it. Well aware how people can be consumed with envy, he depicts the monster as living in self-torture. The fangs of a serpent fasten on envy's brow. The flames about his feet are about to burn him and his world.

✳

The staff in the Tourist Office in Stratford had difficulty keeping a smile off their faces when an American couple asked for directions to Shakespeare's manger! I wonder if these same tourists also confused the caskets in Shakespeare's *Merchant of Venice* – the gold, silver and lead caskets, with the caskets brought by the Wise Men.

What profound insights Shakespeare's casket scenes reveal about the human heart. The suitor who chose the casket containing Portia's picture was to receive Portia's hand in marriage. On the gold casket her father had inscribed the words, '*Who chooseth me shall gain what many men desire*'. On the silver casket, '*Who chooseth me shall get as much as he deserves*', and on the lead casket, '*Who chooseth me must give and hazard all he has*'. At first the choice of casket might seem like a lottery, the mere toss of a coin or dice, but in fact it was so much more than that. Portia's father was well aware there are men whose prime concern is their own pleasure, men for whom everything is determined on the basis of self-interest, men who even marry for self-interest, men for whom the $64,000 dollar question is, 'Where do you get $64,000 dollars'. Portia's father suspected that the gold casket would appeal to such. '*Who chooseth me shall gain what many men desire*'. The Prince of Morocco was just such a person, though he might have described his approach to life as 'utilitarian self-regard', his philosophy was essentially, 'I love me and I want you'. Not surprisingly he chose the gold casket, but Portia's portrait was not there.

Portia's father also knew there are men who have a swollen idea of their own importance, people who are eager to be rewarded according to merit, for they are convinced they merit a great deal. Their outlook is that if everybody got what they deserved, the world would be a much happier and better place. It is doubtful if those who think thus have ever done any serious thinking about life at all. What debtors we all are. What did we do to deserve all the unearned riches of home, all the songs and stories of the nursery that with the passing years opened up into the rich heritage of literature and music, the health care that awaited us at our birth, the schools that provided education, the law courts that dispensed justice? One can understand why Portia's father did not want a man with an outsize ego for his daughter. Conceited, arrogant people never have been attractive. Portia's father suspected that the man who came convinced he was offering Portia more than he would ever get in return, would choose the silver casket with the inscription, '*Who chooseth me shall get as much as he deserves*.' The Prince of Arogan was such a person. He chose the silver casket, but Portia's portrait was not there.

Portia's father knew, however, that there are other men who are more concerned about giving than getting, men prepared to go the second mile and do the bit over for those they love. He perhaps recalled the sacrifices Portia's mother had made for her, the long days and nights spent nursing a sick child.

> *Love ever gives, forgives, outlives*
> *Ever stands with open hands*
> *And while it lives, it gives*
> *For this is love's prerogative*
> *To give and give and give.*

Portia's father wanted such a caring husband for his daughter. He believed the third inscription, '*Who chooseth me must give and hazard all he has*', would strike a chord with just such a person. It certainly appealed to Bassanio. The prize was his.

❈

On a wayside pulpit I once saw an unusual notice. 'Don't just do something. Sit there.' Living as many of us do in cities which are anthills of frantic activity, we need from time to time to be alone with our thoughts, to reflect upon what it means to be human. Without such reflection life can easily become little more than a feast of buzz. Times of quiet are as necessary for spiritual health as vitamins are for bodily health. The naturalist Henry Thoreau said that although he had no drawing room, he had a 'withdrawing room'.

❈

Solitude is necessary, but we also need people to whom we can whisper, 'Solitude is necessary'. The human heart craves companionship. We become fully human only in relationship with others. It is in such relationships that our personalities grow. Whereas solitude expresses the glory of being alone, loneliness expresses the pain of being alone. One Friday evening I met a man who had recently lost his wife. He was carrying a bunch of flowers, upside down, as men tend to do. When I mentioned the flowers the man smiled and said, 'I felt I had to buy them today. You see each Friday when my wife was alive I took her home some flowers.' Later that night I saw a light in the man's lounge. I pictured him sitting there alone, with his flowers almost certainly just stuck into a vase. That started me thinking about the many lonely people who understand what Queen Victoria meant when she said after the death of Prince Albert, 'There is no one to call me Victoria now', and what Jean-Paul Sartre meant when he wrote, 'Without a looker-on, a person evaporates.'

❋

A cartoon depicted an unshaven, sad-eyed old man looking into a mirror. To his image he was saying, 'You are all I have got.' Solitary confinement is such an awful punishment that only in extreme cases are prisoners subjected to it. And yet outside our prisons many are effectively living in solitary confinement. They are alone, not one day, but every day. Terry Waite's experience as a hostage gave him a deeper understanding of those who are hostages as a result of ill-health, those confined for years to the same four walls. After his release Terry Waite spoke feelingly of those brave people who each morning wake to face another day of physical weakness and confinement with little support. He said, 'Unlike political hostages whose stories gain worldwide attention, the struggles and plight of many of these casualties in our society go unnoticed.'

❋

In Charles Dickens' *Christmas Carol* the miseries of Scrooge's life led up to his final and possibly greatest misery. He sees himself dying alone and unmourned. I become more and more convinced that the greatest threat life holds for many is not poverty, or illness, or thwarted ambition, but loneliness. A social worker tells of visiting an elderly lady. On almost every page of her diary was the heartrending entry, 'No one called today.' Another social worker tells of an old man she came across who had more than thirty clocks in his room. Twenty-two were actually ticking. Since his wife had died hardly anyone had come to see him. He spoke to his clocks as he wound them up. Such prolonged loneliness can turn the rich soil of the spirit into a desert. It has driven many to an unhealthy dependency on alcohol and some to suicide.

❋

Lorraine Hansberry in her powerful play, *A Raisin in the Sun*, tells of a black family that lived in Chicago's South-side. Shortly after the father died, their mother inherited ten thousand dollars from an insurance policy. The mother wanted to use the money to fulfil one of her fondest dreams, which was to move her family into a little house in a better part of Chicago. The problem was that her son wanted the money to set up in business. Never before had he had a chance to do this. A friend of his who had heard of the insurance policy convinced him that with that kind of money they could make a start in business, and make a lot of money. Then he would be able to do all kinds of fine things for his mother and family. The mother finally gives in to her son's pleadings. How could she deny her son the opportunity to do something worthwhile with his life. So she gives him half the money. In the next scene we learn that the son's friend has taken the money and hastily left town. With bowed head and slumped shoulders, the son comes and confesses what has happened. His sister Beneatha wastes no time in telling him exactly what she thinks of him. She condemns him for being such a fool. She screams at him for having squandered the only escape route for the family from the ghetto in which they had lived for years. When she finishes her furious tirade, the mother speaks: 'I thought I taught you to love each other.' 'Love him,' Beneatha shouts back. 'There is nothing left to love.' 'Beneatha,' says her mother, 'there is always something left to love. And if you ain't learned that, you ain't learned nothing... When do you think is the time to love somebody the most; when they done good and made things easy for everyone? No... It is when a person's at his lowest and can't believe in himself any more.' Such undeserved love is the meaning of grace. It is a word of life and a remedy for many heart problems. Would that more of us allowed forgiveness to act as a lightning rod, grounding hostilities; would that we were willing to say to ourselves, 'The hostility stops here.'

✳

In 1986 a New York Rabbi, David Blumenfeld, visited Jerusalem with a party of tourists. During the visit they were attacked by members of the Palestine Liberation Organisation. Some of his party were killed. He himself was seriously wounded by a bullet which struck him in the head. His daughter Laura, who was a student at Harvard at the time, coped with the tragedy by writing a poem in which she promised one day to wreak revenge on her father's assailant. Twelve years later, in her capacity as a journalist with the *Washington Post*, she decided to write a book about revenge. She went to Israel and studied the court records. Discovering that her father's assailant Omar Kathib was still in prison, she began a correspondence with him. Omar admitted that it was a tourist he had shot. He also told her in his letters what it had been like to grow up in the occupied West Bank. On reading this, her feelings towards him began to mellow. When a hearing was finally scheduled to discuss his possible release, Laura decided to fly to Jerusalem and attend the hearing. She surprised many when she rose to speak — in Hebrew. She told the court that the victim Rabbi David Blumenfeld was her father, and that he urged clemency. In the book which she finally completed, *Revenge: A Story of Hope*, she tells how she had gradually learned the wisdom of the old Arab saying, 'If you are planning revenge on someone, you had better dig two graves; one for your victim and another for yourself.' Another of her incisive comments is: 'When you really take time to look someone in the eye, it becomes very hard to shoot him in the head.'

✻

During the American Civil War, desertion from the Union Army was an offence punishable by death. Roswell McIntyre committed this offence. At his trial he admitted his guilt. Although he promised that if he was given a second chance he would be loyal, he was sentenced to death. Only a presidential pardon could save him. Out of pity for the young lad, and touched by his promise, President Lincoln not only pardoned him, but wrote out a pass for him to return to his regiment.

Executive Mansion October 4 1864

Upon condition that Roswell McIntyre of the Sixth Regiment of New York Cavalry, returns to his regiment and faithfully serves out his term, making up for lost time or until otherwise discharged, he is fully pardoned for any supposed desertion, and this paper is his pass to go back to his regiment.

A. Lincoln.

In the government records in Washington this paper is preserved, with the following notation across the outside: 'Taken from the body of R. McIntyre at the battle of the Five Forks, Virginia, 1865.'

The Power of Words

Words fascinate me. No modern tool or invention is as magical, mysterious or powerful as words. You wag a piece of red muscle in your jaws, and by doing so set sound waves moving. A small receiving set in another person's ear picks up the vibrations and by an incredible miracle translates them into meaning. It is no different with written words. I once watched a television programme about a Mary Grayson, a music teacher in England who corresponded with Ray Clarke, a prisoner in death row in a Florida prison. She sat at her desk in England, moved her pen over a piece of paper, folded the paper and posted it. Ray Clarke's final months before he was executed were totally transformed by receiving these letters. He was deeply moved and comforted by the genuine love and concern her words communicated.

A professor of English one day got to thinking about a teacher he once had who had instilled in him a love of the English language and poetry. Discovering that she was still alive, he wrote her a letter expressing his thanks. In her reply she said, '*I cannot tell you how much your note meant to me. I am in my eighties now, living alone in a small room, cooking my own meals, lonely and rather like the last leaf of autumn, lingering behind. You may be interested to note that I taught school for almost 50 years, and yours is one of the few notes of appreciation I have received. It came on a cold morning and it cheered me as nothing has in years.*'

'You are looking lovely... I like your hairstyle... What a delightful meal that was... How well you played... ' Such complimentary words can greatly enrich a person's life, can rekindle enthusiasm and spur the hearer to greater effort. Lord Tennyson once commented on the genius of the young Rudyard Kipling. Years later Kipling said about Tennyson's commendation, 'When the private in the ranks is praised by the general... he fights the better the next day." Mark Twain would have agreed. He said, 'I can live for two months on a compliment.'

President Calvin Coolidge was a man of few words. One night at a dinner the lady sitting next to him told him that she had bet a friend that she could get more than three words out of him. On hearing this Coolidge is reported to have said, 'Madam, you lose.' He then retreated back into himself. He did this so often that when the news one day reached Dorothy Parker that Coolidge had died, she inquired, 'How do they know? He did not speak when alive.' How different it was with a woman I once knew. She spoke 140 words to the minute, with gusts of up to 180. The only time she stopped talking was when her mother started.

✳

Edwin Muir, the Orkney poet, was brought up in a very Calvinistic atmosphere. Sunday services were extremely long, some wordy ministers being known to preach for more than an hour. Writing years later of these services, he said, 'The Word which became flesh, has become words again.'

✳

Though sticks and stones can break our bones, words can make our blood boil. They can also leave wounds which take longer to heal than broken bones. A child's worst memories are often about words that hurt their feelings — a classmate's comment about their appearance, a sarcastic remark of a teacher, or the offhand remark of a parent which the parent cannot now remember.

✳

Words can so easily be misused and abused. When one of the government's most illustrious spin-doctors was overheard to bemoan a biased media, it seemed like a burglar bemoaning the fact that his own home had been broken into.

✳

How often pleasant euphemistic words have masked awful actions. The Nazis spoke of finding a *Final Solution* to the Jewish problem, by which they actually meant committing every Jewish man, woman and child to the gas ovens. How mathematically inoffensive the words 'final solution' sound, but how monstrously depraved the solution. Admirers of Stalin spoke approvingly of the 'liquidation of recalcitrant elements'. It makes you think initially of chemistry labs and Bunsen burners, instead of brains splattered over prison floors. Writing of the contamination of words, George Orwell pointed out how euphemisms can persuade people to endorse unspeakable horrors which would normally sicken them.

*

For good or ill most things are started with words. To speak of mere words is like speaking of mere dynamite. Hitler's words captivated and demonised a whole nation. A striking painting depicts Hitler in his early Munich days, before he and his demonic gang seized power. In the picture Hitler is depicted addressing a group of his fanatically devoted followers, who are hanging on every impassioned syllable he uttered. The picture bears a title which might be thought blasphemous, but which conveys a truth too profound to be so dismissed. 'In the beginning was the Word'. It is however also true that most of those who shaped human destiny for the better were also masters of the written and spoken word. With what clarity, grandeur and passion people like Socrates, Jesus, Shakespeare, Dickens, Lord Shaftesbury, Winston Churchill, Martin Luther King... used words.

*

Speech is the most natural way of showing love, care and concern. In many spheres of life trouble develops when the talking stops, when parents, teenagers and neighbours no longer speak, when husband and wife no longer communicate, when in industry the talking stops, when nations leave the conference table, or break off diplomatic relations. Caring love cannot then get a word in.

*

We use metaphor, live or dead every day of our lives. We describe someone as being 'green with envy', or a 'pain in the neck'. Teenagers returning from a disco or a pop concert, sometimes say, 'It was magic' or 'It was out of this world'. A mother tells her friend how her daughter came home in a 'flood of tears'. None of these phrases are literally true, but they convey quickly and pretty accurately an idea which is readily understood. How I wish people realised that it is no different with great literature. From first page to last, the Bible is full of metaphors and word pictures. These are to be taken seriously, but not literally. In Shakespeare's *As You Like It*, we are told there are 'tongues in trees, books in running brooks, sermons in stones'. Though that statement is not true literally, it highlights the truth that many lessons can be learned from the natural world. A factually minded proofreader might well have tried to set Shakespeare straight by revising it to read, 'trunks in trees, stones in running brooks and sermons

39

in books'. Though these statements would be factually true, they would communicate no important truth about the world around us.

The conversation of many people involves recycling not much more than a hundred words. It was no different with Shakespeare. Although his plays contain almost thirty thousand different words, no more than a hundred make up fifty percent of the texts. The wonder of Shakespeare's plays is the magic he produced by mixing in the other words.

Someone once defined a cocktail party as a time when we eat savouries and nibble away at other people's reputations. Far more people are run down by gossip than by cars. Jewish law considered unkind rumours and malicious gossip worse than stealing, because when an item is stolen there is always the possibility of recovering it, or being financially compensated. But a besmirched reputation, as Shakespeare also knew, is not so easily restored. '*Who steals my purse steals trash; 'tis something, nothing. 'Twas mine, 'tis his, and has been slave to thousands; But he that filches from me my good name, robs me of that which not enriches him, and makes me poor indeed.*' These wise words highlight the measure of our frailty and shame. I just wish they had not come from the mouth of Shakespeare's loathsome villain, Iago!

John Hume, the Northern Ireland Nobel Peace Prize winner, tells how he once told Ian Paisley that if they took 'no' out of the language, he would be rendered silent. Ian Paisley retorted, 'No I wouldn't.'

Towards the end of his acting career, one of Britain's most distinguished actors occasionally had too much to drink before going on stage. This sometimes made him unsure of his words. On one occasion, not getting the prompt he wanted, he staggered to the wings of the theatre and hissed, 'What's the line?' The much abused prompter, deciding it was time for revenge, replied, 'What's the play?'

'Short words are best,' said Churchill, 'and the old words are best of all.' Many clergymen and magazine editors unfortunately think otherwise. They seem to prefer big words to shorter ones.

Begin — commence
Buy — purchase
Go — proceed
Live — reside
Meet — gather or foregather
Praise — pay tribute
Rain — inclement weather

They are also often guilty of not using one word if they can use several.

Thank — express deep gratitude
Pray — make fervent intercession for
End — draw to a close
Discuss — give consideration to the question of
Before — prior to the commencement of
Act — take the necessary steps
Now — as at this moment in time

Has it ever struck you how violent are some of the terms we use. We execute a will; smother a sneeze; steal a glance; kill an urge; burn our boats.

Words constantly change their meaning. Unfortunately the tendency is for their meaning to be downgraded rather than upgraded. Crafty originally meant adept at one's craft. Now it means wily, not really to be trusted. Plausible originally meant deserving of applause. Now it suggests something specious. When the king was being shown round the rebuilt St Paul's Cathedral in London, he said to the architect. 'It is awful. It is artificial. It is amusing... ' The architect was thrilled, for in these days awful meant 'full of awe', artificial meant 'made of art', and amusing meant 'amazing'.

In the graveyard of an old village church, an epitaph concerning a former minister reads, 'He was vicar of this parish, without ever showing the least sign of enthusiasm.' When that epitaph was carved, the word 'enthusiasm', meant a kind of frenzy or fanaticism. What the epitaph was in fact saying was that the old vicar had been a steady character who did not panic. Another old tombstone, this time for a Western Isles minister, tells us that he was a 'laborious preacher'. Laborious originally meant hard-working and well prepared.

✳

As a young man the Rt Hon George Reid, the Presiding Officer of the Scottish Parliament, worked as a reporter for his local Alloa newspaper. Being an Alloa Athletic supporter. he was thrilled to be asked to report on the Celtic–Alloa Cup tie. Celtic having won 6–1, one national newspaper carried the headline 'Alloa hit for six'. George on the other hand chose for the heading to his report, 'Alloa and Celtic in 7-goal thriller.'

✳

Whereas some people have a great facility with words, others have great difficulty communicating their thoughts. I am certain that here we have the root cause of some of the violence in our society. Whereas we argue with words, others feel unable to do this. So they argue with their fists. The fury of the inarticulate. Letters written to Social Security offices, car insurance companies, teachers and agony aunts reveal the difficulty many people have in expressing what they really mean.

In accordance with your instructions, you will see that I gave birth to twins in the enclosed envelope.

A lorry driver who had hit a cyclist sought to describe what had happened. 'I tried to go slow, but could not go slow fast enough to stop in time.'

A driver involved in an accident, in his letter to the Insurance Company, gave the impression that he had three eyes, 'I had one eye on a parked car, another on an approaching lorry and another on the woman behind.'

Another letter accompanying an insurance claim read, 'I am happy to announce that my husband who was reported missing, is now definitely deceased.'

A letter to a Glasgow teacher read, 'The reason Johnnie has not been at school is that he has had diarrhoea, through a hole in his shoe.' The mind boggles.

A minister friend tells of standing one day near an elevator in a brand new hospital. Suddenly his eye was drawn to a sign partly visible round the corner. It read, 'AGNOSTIC SERVICES'. Curious as to whether the hospital, as well as having a chaplain, had started some kind of counselling programme for the non believer and non-committed, he approached the corner to see the sign again. From his new vantage point, he discovered it read, 'DIAGNOSTIC SERVICES'.

✳

When John McEnroe got upset on the tennis court, a not uncommon occurrence, his language deteriorated considerably. A clever advert for the brand of tennis shoes he wore had the telling caption: 'McEnroe swears by them.' The mind's ear fooling as it often does the body's eye, I am sure many thought it read, 'McEnroe swears in them'.

✳

I love humour that is a play on words and well-known phrases.

Those responsible for a charity ramble, separated the participants into groups according to age and walking ability: 1–3 years – Pramblers; 4–10 years – Scramblers; 11–70 years – Ramblers; 70–90 years – Amblers; 90 and over – Gamblers.

A woman tells how her father's pride and joy was his vegetable garden. Arriving for dinner one Sunday he brought a box full of tomatoes and carrots. A card attached read, 'The last rows of summer.'

Though a brillant scientist, Lord Kelvin was by no means the best lecturer in Glasgow University. The day he received his knighthood from the Queen, his assistant Mr Day quoted to his students some words from John's Gospel. 'Work while it is *day*; for the *night* cometh when no man can work.'

During an African tour, one tribe wanted to bring out the ceremonial throne for Princess Margaret to sit on. The problem was that when they got it out of the hut it crumbled. It had been eaten by white ants. The Princess' speech-writer suggested that at a dinner that night, she should include an altered version of the well-known English proverb, 'People who live in grass houses shouldn't stow thrones.' I have been unable to find out whether the Princess accepted his suggestion.

A sign painted on a very old van read, 'The Ugly Truckling'.

It is always dullest before the yawn.

The early bird may get the worm, but it is the second mouse that gets the cheese.

He never let the sun go down on his anger, but there were some colourful sunsets.

To the question, what is the difference between ignorance and apathy, the reply was, 'I don't know and I don't care'.

✳

Some jokes which are a play on words make you groan and laugh at the same time. Five examples will more than suffice!

One Christmas Eve, two Russian peasants Ivan and his wife Olga, were having an argument as they walked home. Like many marital disputes it was over a minor matter. Ivan thought it was raining. Olga was sure it was snowing. Meeting Rudolph, the leader of the local communist party, they agreed to get him to settle their argument. When Rudolph said it was raining, not snowing, Olga was still not convinced. Look said Ivan, '*Rudolph the Red knows rain dear*'!!

✳

What did Adam say to his wife the day before Christmas? 'It is Christmas, Eve.'

✳

A father willed his prize collection of 343 clocks to his son. We are told the son spent the rest of his life winding up the estate!

✳

What does a portrait by Picasso have in common with a vote in the House of Commons – 'Ayes to the right. Noes to the left.'

✳

What did the Israeli ski-racer say when she hung up her skis for the last time? 'Shalom, slalom.'

Seriously Funny

Adolescence — that period when people start things they can't finish, like phone-calls.

Age — something a woman keeps to herself because a man rarely acts his.

Anatomy — something that looks much better on a girl.

Bachelor — a man with an un-altar-able view.

Bank — where they lend you an umbrella in fair weather and ask for it back when it begins to rain.

Celibacy — a characteristic that was not inherited.

Charm — what people have until they begin to rely upon it.

Christmas meals — a few moments on your lips, a lifetime on your hips.

Church nave — a youngster who runs about during the service.

Clear conscience — sign of a bad memory.

Comedy — a way of being seriously funny.

Conclusion — the place where you get tired of thinking.

Courtship — the period during which a girl decides whether or not she can do better.

Desk — a waste-basket with drawers.

Economist — one whose guess is as good as anyone else's.

Family budget — a process of cheques and balances, the cheques wiping out the balances.

Fundamentalism — religion that has too little fun, too much damn, and not enough mentalism.

Garden — a thing of beauty and a job forever.

Girl — a woman of your own age.

Horse-sense — what horses have that keep them from betting on people.

Intellectual — one who uses more words than necessary to tell more than he knows.

Middle Age — that part of life half-way between adolescence and obsolescence.

Minutes — the collective half-truths the committee have agreed to tell.

Modern Music — the kind where if you make a mistake, no one notices.

Napkin — a group of relatives taking a siesta together.

Nonchalance — the ability to look like an owl when you have behaved like an ass.

Obesity — living beyond your seams.

Old age — the high price we pay for maturity.

Omnipresent — a gift for all occasions.

Parents — the bones upon which children cut their teeth.

Patience — what we most need when we run out of it.

Pessimist's blood-type — B-negative.

Politeness — the most acceptable form of hypocrisy.

Politician — a man full of promise.

Probus — a play-group for grandpas.

Proverb — a crystal of wisdom left at the bottom of the crucible of human experience.

Purgatory — Hell's non-smoking section.

Retired husband — a wife's fulltime job.

Righteous Anger — jealousy with a halo.

Running mate — a husband who dared to talk back.

Saint — a dead sinner revised and edited.

Skiing — the next best thing to having wings.

Today — the tomorrow you worried about yesterday.

Virus — Latin word used by doctors to mean 'Your guess is as good as mine.'

Beans in their Ears

Children are both lovable and bewildering. They exhaust their parents as well as delighting them. In the musical *Fantastiko*, two fathers sing about what it is like to have children.

> Why do kids put beans in their ears?
> No one can hear with beans in their ears.
> After a while the reason appears
> They did it 'cause we said 'No'.

✳

A mother tells how shortly after her 3-year old daughter started nursery school, she came rushing home, proudly clutching a beautifully decorated Mother's Day card. 'That is wonderful,' her mother said. 'Do you know I have never had a Mother's Day card before.' 'Well,' she replied, holding the card tightly, 'you are not getting mine.'

✳

In his *Prayer of the Selfish Child*, Shel Silverstein amends a well known prayer to remind his readers that sharing does not come naturally to young children.

> *Now I lay me down to sleep*
> *I pray the Lord my soul to keep*
> *And if I die before I wake*
> *I pray the Lord my toys to break*
> *So no other kids can use them!*

Young children have to be taught to share. Doing so is an important step toward civilisation.

✳

I often wonder why people say, 'You have a baby.' It would be nearer the truth to say, 'The baby has you.' Has it ever struck you how a tiny baby would be the most terrifying creature on earth if he had the strength of a man, for his sole concern is getting what he wants?

✳

For many years Ewan Dawson worked with children. He told of one 10-year-old boy who had plasters from above the knees to the ankles to keep them stiff. After a couple of days he was back with the plasters broken. After another few days he was back again with broken plasters. His explanation. 'We play cricket and I'm the wickets.'

During a maths lesson, the teacher wrote some fractions on the blackboard. He then explained that the numerator was the top part of the fraction, and the denominator the bottom. Leaning back against the blackboard, he asked the pupils if they had any questions. A minute later when he turned round to write on the blackboard, laughter filled the room. 'Sir,' one pupil called out, 'you have chalk dust all over your denominator.'

✳

The cartoonist Bill Keane tells of the time he was drawing one of his cartoons. His son Jeffrey asked, 'Daddy, how do you know what to draw?' When he replied, 'God tells me,' his son asked, 'Why then do you keep erasing parts?'

✳

Those familiar with computers will appreciate the story of the pupil who when he was asked by the teacher why his handwriting was not as neat as usual, said he was trying out a new 'font'.

✳

A little boy running down the street turned a corner suddenly and collided with a man. 'My goodness,' said the man, 'where are you off to in such a hurry?' 'Home,' said the wee lad. 'I'm in a hurry because my mother is going to give me a row.' 'Are you so eager to get a row that you are running home for it?' asked the astonished stranger. 'No. But if my Dad gets home before me, he will give me an even bigger row.'

✳

A mother of three small boys tells how she was preparing for a dinner party. Several months previously she had reluctantly agreed to the boys getting a dog. Late in the afternoon when the boys were playing a rather boisterous game with the dog, her favourite lounge lamp came crashing to the floor. 'Get to your room,' she shouted. 'Either the dog goes or I go.' As the boys made their way upstairs, she overheard one of them whisper, 'It is not fair. Dad will make us choose her.'

✳

When a boy was asked what were the advantages of mother's milk over against other forms of milk, he replied, 'It is cheaper, and the cat can't get it.'

✳

In an essay about the harmful effects of oil pollution on sea life, one boy wrote, 'Last night my mother opened a tin of sardines. It was full of oil and all the sardines were dead.'

✳

A mother recalls how when she was a little girl attending primary school in the 1960s, her teacher, a Miss Stringer, about whom she still has occasional nightmares, would not let her be an angel in the school nativity play. 'Angels don't wear glasses,' said Miss Stringer firmly. When she was finally cast as an ox, she audibly commented to her friend that she had never seen an ox with glasses. Unfortunately the teacher overheard her and made her write out a hundred times, 'I must not talk back to the teacher.' Poor wee lass.

✳

Ron Ferguson was born and educated in Cowdenbeath in Fife. As a boy he was regularly to be found on a Saturday afternoon on the terracing at Central Park. To this day he is still a loyal supporter of Blue Brazil, the glorious nickname of the Cowdenbeath soccer team. Each Saturday he eagerly listens on the radio for the Cowdenbeath score. During his years as minister of St Magnus Cathedral in Orkney, he would sometimes make a passing reference to Cowdenbeath in his talk to the children. A mother once told him how, on their way home from church, her son had asked, 'Why does Mr Ferguson speak so often about Cows and Beef?'

✳

A boy who arrived late for Sunday School explained he had hoped to go fishing with his Dad, but his Dad at the last minute had said he should go to Sunday School. The teacher then asked if his Dad had told him why it was more important for him to go to church? 'Yes, he did not have enough bait for us both.'

✳

I have often wondered, what message a school answering service might carry, if it followed the pattern of British Rail or BT. Would it be something like this?

In order to assist you, please listen to all options.

To lie about why your child is absent — press 1

To make excuses for your child not doing his/her homework — press 2

To complain about what some teacher has done or said — press 3

To request a change of teacher for more than the 3rd time — press 4

To inform us your child is an angel and couldn't possibly have done anything wrong — Press 5

✻

A psychologist conducted an experiment with children regarding instant gratification. He gave a group of four-year-olds a choice. If they wanted a marshmallow they could have it now. But if they wanted two marshmallows they would have to wait until he ran an errand. He told them he would be gone for about twenty minutes. How each of the children responded was recorded. Many years later the participants, by then teenagers, were located. The emotional and social differences between those who grabbed the marshmallow and those who delayed gratification was dramatic. Those who delayed gratification were more socially competent, more reliable, self-assured and better able to cope with stress and frustrations.

✻

A Glasgow man tells how at their Roman Catholic Church the primary school pupils attend mass once a month. Before one of the services the teachers had told them to speak up at the responses. When the priest paused at the altar and said, 'There is something wrong with this microphone,' two hundred young voices bellowed, 'And also with you.'

✻

A young child was 'acting up' in church. The parents did their best to maintain some sense of order in the pew, but were losing the battle. Finally the father grabbed the little fellow by the arm and marched him up the centre aisle. There was a stern look on the father's face. Just before reaching the door the wee lad called loudly to the congregation, 'Pray for me. Pray for me.'

✻

When a father was asked what his son was going to be when he finally left university, he replied, 'An old man.'

✻

A man tells of attending a meeting. Part of the programme was to watch a video, which would be discussed later. Unfortunately no one was able to get the video recorder to work. Raising his hand for silence, the chairman asked, 'Is there a six-year-old in the house?'

✳

When mothers have a headache they should do what it says on the aspirin bottle: 'Take two and keep away from children'!

✳

A grandfather was reading his grandson Neil the story of Noah's Ark. 'Were you in the Ark?' asked the wee lad. When the grandfather laughingly replied, 'No', Neil then asked, 'Then why weren't you drowned?'

✳

During the Christmas celebrations in the Douglas home in Stirlingshire, the youngest member of the family decided it was all too much. Elbowing her way through the adult revellers, she emerged in the kitchen. There she revealed her grasp of the Christmas story by announcing: 'It is too crowded in there – just like Bethlehem.'

✳

The Rev Susan Brown, the minister of Dornoch Cathedral, is not often at a loss for words, but she was at a recent Christmas day family service. With her portable microphone, she asked some of the children what special present they had got for Christmas. All went well until one little lad said, 'A virgin.' Pretending she had not heard the first time, and hoping he would correct his mistake, she asked him again. When for the second time he said, 'A virgin,' his embarrassed mother called out, 'A Virgin train.'

✳

Comments in school report cards can sometimes be very amusing. A geography teacher wrote, 'John does well to find his way home.' An English teacher wrote, 'The improvement in the legibility of Mary's handwriting is revealing serious deficiencies in her spelling.'

✳

A four-year-old boy was out walking with his grandmother on a bitterly cold morning. His breath came from his nose and mouth like fine white smoke. 'Granny,' he explained happily, 'look at my exhaust.'

The 4-year-old cried on the way home after the baptism of his little sister. When his Dad asked what was the matter, the wee boy sobbed, 'The minister said he wanted us to be brought up in a Christian home, but I want to stay with you and Mum.'

✳

A Mrs Hutchins tells how she once held up a picture of Jesus riding into Jerusalem on the first Palm Sunday. From the back of the class a little voice said, 'How he's grown since Christmas.'

✳

When the Sunday School teacher asked the children if they loved God, they all said, 'Yes.' But when she next asked them why they loved God, they were silent, until one little boy said, 'I think it runs in the family.'

✳

Being childlike is very different from being infantile or gullible. Childlike vision belongs to open minds, receptive ears and bright eyes. A mother tells how her little boy used to wake up in the morning and say, 'Wow'. Then she added, 'What saddens me is that I suspect, like so many of us, he will eventually wake up one day only to say "ugh". I wish I knew what I could do to prevent this ever happening.'

✳

A. A. Milne paints a delightful picture of a child's amazing curiosity and powers of observation. The child who reels off a list of the most marvellous things, is told to 'run along' by grown-ups who seemed to belong to the Society for the Suppression of Astonishment.

> *There's sun on the river and sun on the hill:*
> *You can hear the sea if you stand quite still*
> *There's eight new puppies at Roundabout farm*
> *And I saw an old sailor with only one arm*
> *But everyone says, 'Run along. Run along.'*

'Run along dear' can be deadly words. Like a blighting frost they can stunt the child's growing imagination. How life is impoverished when the vision splendid fades in a child's eye, when the child's inquiring mind is dulled.

An author once gave some reasons why he prefers writing for children than adults

— Children read books, not reviews

— They don't give a hoot about the critics

— They love interesting stories, not commentaries, guides or footnotes

— When a book is boring, they yawn openly without any shame

One day as I drove past a house which was worth a fortune, I noticed a little girl playing in the large garden. She was wearing an expression of total pleasure. It had been raining and there were puddles of muddy water. Having collected some twigs and pieces of gravel, she was splashing in the water, building a dam, launching a ship. She was altogether happy as she got her designer jeans and trainers soaking wet and filthy. What she had found to do, she was doing with all the enthusiasm, interest and energy at her command. When it comes to real fun, children's happiest moments are found, not in costly games or pleasures, but in those they make for themselves, with such simple things as puddles of rainwater.

A couple were entertaining friends for dinner. Their five-year-old daughter helped to serve the dessert. When she brought the first slice of tart, she laid it in front of her Dad. He politely passed it to the woman on his right. When she returned with the second portion and again placed it in front of her Dad, she watched him doing the same thing — passing it to another female guest. 'Dad,' she said, 'you might as well keep it. They are all the same size.'

Whenever a child can be seen and not heard, it is a shame to wake him.

The little boy showed his baby-sitter the family photo-album. When he pointed to a picture of his whole family, the baby-sitter complimented him on how handsome he looked. He shook his head and said, 'I don't think my Mum likes this picture. She says she wants to have it blown up.'

The audience at the circus watched nervously as the knives surrounded the thrower's attractive assistant. One little boy was however unimpressed. 'The knives are missing her every time.'

✳

According to the children's joke, the longest word in the English language is SMILES, there being a 'mile' between the first letter of S–MILE–S and the last. This old joke came to mind when my son Alistair, who works for Ethicon, the surgical subsidiary of the pharmaceutical giant Johnson and Johnson, gave me to read a signed copy of a wonderful book he had been given, entitled, *Changing Lives One Smile at a Time*. The book, by Dr Bill Magee, the founder of Operation Smile, was dedicated to 'All the wonderful people at Ethicon. Thanks for your kindness and generosity over these past 20 years. Over 70,000 children thank you for allowing them to smile.' Operation Smile is an organisation that crosses national and cultural barriers to bring facial reconstruction surgery to medically needy youngsters. One of the most moving stories in the book is about Li Xingshan, a 51-year-old beggar, who during a visit to a smelly rubbish heap in Hubei, China, found a tiny baby lying motionless in a cardboard box, too weak to cry, a bottle of milk at her side. As he looked at the infant's face it became clear why her family had abandoned her. She was what some Chinese call a rabbit child, a baby born with a cleft lip and palate. It being an old Chinese superstition that rabbit children are an evil omen, portending famine, poverty or death, it is not surprising that such children are often abandoned. The beggar fed her from the bottle. He returned the following day and fed her again. He hoped that someone would find her and take her home. But nobody did. On the third day the beggar reluctantly decided to take her home. But his wife wanted to have nothing to do with her. She insisted he take her back to the dump. This he refused to do. She then told him to leave. He did, taking the baby with him. He called her Li Mengfang, which means 'dreaming of being normal'. For several years he wandered through China sustaining himself and his little girl by begging and scrounging for cans and bottles for which he got a little money. They eventually ended up in the province of Shantou where he found, on another rubbish dump, a leaflet about Operation Smile. He went and pled with the doctors to help the little girl he loved so dearly. The surgeons still recall his gratitude after what was a successful operation, an operation that made it possible for the little girl to smile. 'You have given me everything I could ask for in life.'

A Single for the Wife

Near to London Underground's Embankment station there appeared a large poster depicting Henry VIII standing at a ticket office saying, 'Tower Hill, please.' Some wag had written underneath, 'And a single for the wife.'

❋

When in the vestry after the wedding the minister said to the groom, a Gary Young, 'You may now kiss Mrs Young,' the groom turned and kissed his mother.

❋

Everybody marries for 'love'. The problem is that if what we love most is money or position or looks, or pleasure-seeking, then for better or worse this is the love a marriage is based on.

❋

Outside a shop in Ontario was a board on which had been written 'Wedding dress for sale — only once used — by mistake!'

❋

Coming across the word 'infanticide' in his newspaper, a husband commented to his wife, who was trying to follow a difficult knitting pattern, about the great variety of words used to denote various types of murder — homicide, fratricide, matricide, and so on. When he proceeded to ask her if there was a special word used when a wife murders her husband, without missing a stitch or looking up, she retorted, 'Pesticide.'

❋

When Jean said, 'If mother is going to live with us, we will really have to move to a larger house,' her husband replied, 'It would never work. Sooner or later she would find us.'

❋

In a verse of doggerel an unmarried Glasgow woman made her point forcibly and effectively:

> As a woman I get into a tizz
> On receipt of mail addressed Ms
> I am quite happy with Miss
> And without wedded bliss
> Until Mr Right claims me as Hs

Many who say they are going on a diet are often just wishful shrinkers! Dieting can put strains on the marriage relationship. One husband moaned to his workmates, 'When my wife is dieting she is impossible, and when she is not, she is impassable.'

✱

A woman emerged from the local medical centre to inform her husband that the doctor was certain her chest pains were stress related. When asked what that meant, she said, 'It means that I have to find the source of my stress and get rid of it.' On hearing this, her husband inquired, 'But where will I go?'

✱

No man can consider himself truly married until he understands every word his wife is not saying.

✱

When a husband said to his wife, 'Please tell me if ever I become predictable,' she replied, 'I knew you were going to say that.' Another husband confided to a friend that his wife led a double life — 'hers and mine'. A third marital comment that made me smile was that of a wife concerning dinner. 'Tonight will it be go out, a take out, or thaw out?'

✱

After forty-five years of marriage, my wife can often tell what I am thinking. When I do speak, she can often finish my sentences for me. We are not unique in this. I remember hearing of a wife who asked her husband what he was looking for in the cupboard. When he replied, 'Nothing', she said, 'It is not in there. Look in the top drawer in the bedroom.'

✱

A woman perplexed about a marital problem asked a French colleague, 'How do you know if you have married the wrong man?' Without hesitation, she replied with her heavy French accent, 'It is simple. If you marry ze wrong man you know right away. If you marry ze right man, you never know.'

✱

My wife has lost more single gloves than I care to remember. Had she lost both gloves, I would have been comforted by the thought that at least someone else might have benefited. In this connection

I recall hearing of a woman who noticing one of her new gloves lying on the station platform as the train pulled out, opened the window and threw out the other. How thoughtful.

My problem is not gloves but the high divorce rate among my socks. Why do socks desert their partners? And where do they go? I thought this regular occurrence would stop when our Golden Retriever died. But the mysterious affliction continued. Occasionally the sock would reappear weeks later. But often it never turned up, despite searching the washing machine and the backs of radiators. The only place I did not look was the tumble drier, the reason being we did not have one!

✳

A husband, enjoying a day off work, was watching his wife scurrying about the house. She picked up his dirty clothes, put away his shoes, washed the breakfast dishes, prepared his coffee, and ironed his shirts. Noticing a thoughtful look on his face, she wondered if he was beginning to realise just how much work he created for her. When she finally said, 'A penny for your thoughts,' he replied, 'I was just thinking that one of the things I like best about you is the way you always find something to keep you busy.'

✳

A husband had spent most of Saturday morning washing, waxing and polishing his new car, until every part gleamed. Shortly afterwards his wife asked if, as it had started to rain, he would go and pick up her father from the station. He later admitted that at first he had looked at his wife aghast. 'Take out his newly polished car and get it all splashed?' He found himself making all kinds of excuses — 'The railway station is not really far. The walk would do her Dad good. He could get a taxi... ' But then it suddenly dawned on him what he was doing — putting pride in material possessions above human need. When things cease to serve the good life and become the good life itself, when things coveted and acquired set themselves at the centre of life, rather than the circumference, something has gone wrong.

✳

When Churchill was asked, 'If you could not be you, who would you like to be?' he did not say Julius Caesar or Alexander the Great. He said, 'Lady Churchill's second husband'

The Family Tree

The most basic community is the family. The most important business of one generation is the raising of the next. The decline of family life weakens all other institutions of civil society. If we free children from parental guidance and authority, we expose them even more to the tyranny of their peers. William Homan, a distinguished pediatrician, wrote a letter to a parent who was perplexed about the behaviour of his teenage family. In it he said, ' *Thousands of factors contribute to, and shape the final personality of a growing human being. But in the long run only three are absolutely essential – love, discipline and independence. The good parent is simply one who more than half the time does the right thing instead of the wrong. Of these three fundamentals, the first, caring love, is by far the most important, and it is unique in that there can never be too much. An excess of discipline or too much independence can be harmful. But of true love, the more the better.'*

The oldest word in the English language, unchanged in sound or meaning since human history began, is *Mamma*. Our anatomy is such that when a developing child first makes sounds, that is what comes out. There are no prizes for guessing who grabbed on to it and said proudly, 'That is his name for me.' Well God bless them. If it was not for Mammas we would not be here!

For many years Ralph Reader produced the Scout Gang Show. Each year hundreds of cubs and scouts were on the stage for the finale. At the close of the final rehearsal, one eight-year-old came and said, 'Mr Reader, I have forgotten the tabs for my socks.' Patting him on the head Ralph told him not to worry, that no one would notice. The wee boy begged to differ: 'My Mummy will.'

The Scottish historian Thomas Carlyle told a story of his boyhood. His father on one occasion had to carry him on a narrow plank over a raging stream in full flood. He carried him face downwards with the raging waters in full view. Carlyle's comment in later years was: 'If it had been my mother who carried me, she would have shown me her face.'

A man whose cat often slept on the television claimed that it was one of the wisest creatures he had ever known. He offered three reasons for that evaluation. 1. There is no danger of being stepped on. 2. It is nice and warm. 3. It is the only spot in the room where you can't watch television.

※

When Steven Spielberg's film *ET* was first released, my wife and I took our family to see it. We stood in a queue waiting for those who had been at the earlier showing to come out. When they emerged, the majority were sobbing, some quietly, some not so quietly. I momentarily wondered why, having had such a happy Christmas, we were spending time and money going to a film that would make us sad. The film is about a little creature from a far-off star, who accidentally becomes stranded on earth. He makes friends with a boy called Elliot, and through Elliot with his younger sister and older brother, and later with some of their school friends. Elliot feels he has to protect ET from grown-ups. Whereas he just wanted to love ET and enjoy his friendship, he suspected that grown-ups would want to examine ET, to use him, to explore him as they would an unusual insect. The bond between Elliot and ET grows closer and stronger. He keeps his secret, even from his mother. But she becomes suspicious that something is not quite right. There then follows a sequence of hilarious near-discoveries, the most enchanting of which is when she decides to search Elliot's room. She throws open the toy-cupboard. The camera ranges, as her eye does, along the shelf of cuddly teddy-bears, lions, frogs, and other not so attractive goggle-eyed stuffed animals. Among them, not even blinking, was ET. She fortunately shut the cupboard without seeing him.

The final part of the film begins with an epic struggle – children against adults, bicycles against cars, heart against mind. At the end of an incredible chase, as ET prepares to board the spacecraft, he croaks to Elliot, 'Come with me,' and Elliot whispers, 'Stay with me.' This scene is a real tear-jerker. Both Elliot and ET know that continuing to be together is not a possible option. So they give each other a long, loving embrace. As the loveable little creature ascends the ladder, and the spaceship takes off, painting as it goes the sign of the cross in the heavens, there is not a dry eye in the cinema.

As we drove back home it occurred to me that Spielberg's film is in a strange way a judgement on a consumer-oriented society that encourages us to love things and use people. It is also a commentary on the words of Jesus about who gets the highest rank in God's kingdom. 'Unless you return to square one and start over like children, you are not even going to get a look at the kingdom. Whoever becomes simple and elemental again, like a little child, will rank high in God's kingdom.'

✳

One of the best things a father can do for his children is to go on loving their mother.

✳

When our 13-year-old son flew to Manchester to represent the Highland Region in a Schools Quiz competition, he warned his mother that on no account was she to kiss him goodbye at the airport. Yet, as he left the house, he stopped to give our Golden Retriever a really big hug.

✳

One kangaroo mother said to another, 'Don't you hate those rainy days when they cannot play outside.'

✳

Rabbi Lionel Blue tells how his elderly mother said to him, 'Lionel, I am so pleased you don't have children. They can cause you such pain and anxiety. Believe me. I know.' Lionel's jaw dropped, for he was her only child.

✳

The family had returned from College for the Christmas holidays. Though our large Dornoch manse had six bedrooms, there was only one shower. Each morning there was a race to get there. Two days before Christmas, Neil, the instigator of many a prank, finished up last in the queue. Having often been the butt of his practical jokes, the family decided to get their own back. The moment he was in the shower I turned off the hot water supply. Though Neil emerged quicker than usual, to our amazement he said nothing. But the following day, just before I set off for the BBC studios in Inverness to be Santa in a radio phone-in for children, Neil said, 'Dad, I think I will phone and ask Santa if he could possibly give us a shower with hot water!' The possibility of Neil actually carrying out his threat ruined my morning.

✳

When the second-hand car dealer asked the woman what sort of car she was looking for, she said, 'Preferably something my kids would not be seen dead in.' That story reminded me of the 17-year-old who asked her Dad why he would not let her sit her driving test. 'I am old enough to get a driving licence' 'I know you are,' said her Dad, 'but the car isn't.'

✳

Young people are responsible not only for their parents' worst nightmares, but also their greatest joys. What tear-jerkers school prize-givings and graduation ceremonies can be. A graduation ceremony at Glasgow University and a prize-giving at Tain Royal Academy were for me two such occasions. Gordon Luke's graduation in 1991 was the climax to a heroic story, not the kind that make newspaper headlines, but the kind that is testimony to what can be achieved by incredible courage and dedication, and the support of a loving family and a caring university staff. Shortly after Gordon's second birthday, it was discovered that he was suffering from advanced glaucoma. More than 90% of his sight having been lost, he was from an early age registered blind. My son Alistair, who was of an age with Gordon, and his closest friend, instinctively acted as Gordon's eyes. Our move from Glasgow to Dornoch in 1976 meant that the two boys did not see as much of each other. But the friendship was renewed when both opted to study at Glasgow University. Not only did they graduate the same day, but the two families shared a graduation lunch. Despite having so little sight, Gordon graduated with first-class honours in mathematics. As he was led on to the platform by a university official to be capped, everyone in the Bute Hall rose and applauded. Like his proud parents, my wife and I had a lump in our throats and a tear in our eyes.

The Tain school prize-giving thirteen years later was the climax to another heroic story. The courage and personality of our oldest grandchild, a sufferer from the debilitating Cystic Fibrosis disease, had so endeared Sally to the staff and pupils, that in her final year she was elected school captain by both staff and pupils. When a few months later the rector phoned to ask if I would be the guest speaker at the school prize-giving, I inquired if the invitation had the approval of Sally, for I knew she was due to speak at the ceremony. I would have understood if the last thing she had wanted would have been for her grandfather to share the same platform. On being told that Sally had no objection, I accepted, thanking the head-teacher for the honour. That night Sally phoned and said, 'I believe you have been invited to speak at the prize-giving. Well I want your speech to be absolute rubbish, so that everyone will say how much better his grand-daughter is as a speaker!' What a memorable occasion that prize-giving was. Again my wife and I had a tear in our eyes not only as Sally spoke so wonderfully well, but as she was loudly cheered at the end of her speech.

These two occasions further confirmed my belief that we ought to take special note of those occasions when our voice breaks, and tears come to our eyes, whether they be tears of joy or sorrow or regret, or as in the case of Gordon and Sally, tears of admiration. Such moments are not just formative moments, but often god-moments, moments of insight when we glimpse more clearly what really matters in life, what is true success, and what kind of people most deserve our admiration.

✳

I love the story of John's two grandmothers. About the only thing they had in common was that they both made a big thing of getting ready for Christmas. Grandmother Millar-Craig got her Christmas cake and puddings sent each year from Harrod's. Granny Murray on the other hand managed to convince her grandchildren that chopping nuts and cutting up candied fruit was great fun. Granny Murray's Christmas cake smelled very different from Granny Miller-Craig's. Believing that the Christmas season is the 'season to be jolly', she poured a secret ingredient over the cake mix — to keep it moist! Both Grannies had manger scenes, but again how different. In grandmother Millar-Craig's palatial lounge, there was the most magnificent manger scene. All the figures were made of the finest china. The grandchildren were allowed to look at it, but not to go too near, and certainly not to touch it. Grandmother Murray's manger scene on the other hand had been made by her husband. He had painted the sky himself. There was a little electric light which could be turned on to serve as the Christmas star. Beside the stable was a shoe box filled with the most wonderful assortment of wooden figures. Her grand children and the neighbours' children derived immense joy from arranging and rearranging the figures. As they did so they became part of the story of that remarkable birth in Bethlehem.

✳

When John Logie Baird demonstrated the first TV transmission in the 1920s, a *New York Times* reporter wrote that he was sure television would never be a serious competitor to radio. The article, having pointed out that television requires people to sit and keep their eyes glued to a screen, concluded, 'The average family has not time for that'!

Touching Is Sensational

A man who had a very distinguished brother tells how, during his professional career, he was regularly the victim of the double-handshake. When at a function he was introduced to a stranger as, 'This is Mr... ', the result was often a polite handshake. But when the person introducing him went on to say, 'He is So and So's brother,' he would get a much more forceful handshake.

❋

I remember hearing of a teacher who asked her class to draw something for which they were really thankful. One timid wee soul called Douglas drew a hand. When the teacher inquired whose hand it was, Douglas said, 'It is yours, miss.' Only then did it occur to her how often when the class was going somewhere, to the gym or on a bus outing, she had taken Douglas by the hand. She had thought nothing of it, but what a lot it had meant to Douglas. The clasp of loving arms when thunder rolls, patting a child on the head, dressing and kissing a sore knee – what comfort such touching can provide. Through the medium of touch, touch that has no sexual connotations, the beginning of a cure can be set in motion.

❋

Within every child there is a deep-seated hunger for skin-touch. We need only think of how animals respond to touch. The dog's wagging tail speaks volumes. We used to have a little black and white cat. The family named it 'Boxer' for it had an attractive large black circle round one of his eyes. At night Boxer would jump on your lap. Even before you stroked his back and scratched his chin, he would begin to vibrate. He purred in anticipation of touch. The tragedy is that for some children the only touching they experience is slapping and spanking. Disturbed behaviour patterns in children are often closely linked to sensory deprivation. How wonderful if children could be guaranteed at least one good purring a day.

❋

In her book *Uncle Tom's Cabin* Harriet Beecher Stowe pokes fun at two of her contemporaries who not only defended slavery as a positive good, but had written a Catechism to reinforce the slave's servitude in society. One of the most moving chapters tells how, when Little Eva asks Topsy about her unacceptable behaviour,

Topsy informs her that she might be good if she could somehow 'get out of her black skin'. The little black girl had noticed that Aunt Ophelia, who regularly catechised her about sin, could not bear to touch her. Eva starts the healing process by reaching out and touching her little black friend. Thus she restored her sense of worth.

✳

I have always had a warm feeling for the father of the prodigal son. He had every reason to be hurt by his younger son's irresponsible attitude and conduct. But when his son came home, the father did not just wait at the door. He did not just offer a reluctant handshake. We are told he ran and fell on his son's neck and kissed him. By thus putting his arms round his son, he literally enfolded him with forgiveness.

✳

A well respected medical consultant who worked for many years in a hospice, said to his students, 'If you want to communicate with patients who are dying of cancer, first sit down beside them and take one of their hands in your own. They are then more likely to turn their heads towards you and really listen to what you are saying.'

✳

Response to touch seems to be the first response that is awakened in people, and the last to die. Old people need the comforting and loving touch of hands every bit as much as the young. Long after sight, hearing, speech, mental faculties are lost or impaired, the sense of touch remains. I think of an auxiliary in a Highland geriatric hospital, a middle-aged, over-worked, no nonsense, but very caring person. The qualified nurses had far more medical knowledge and professional skills, yet when Kathleen walked round the wards, often on tired feet, trembling old arms were held out, and quivering voices often called 'Kathleen'. She treated each frail patient with the same respect as she would have her own mother or grandmother. She treated them as she knew she would have wanted to be treated in the unforeseen future, a future which does not always deal us a bed of roses, but sometimes a stroke or a cancer or a degenerative condition. Knowing the heart-hunger and skin-hunger of the old, Kathleen was lavish with her touch. She would hold their hand, or pat their cheeks or wipe their brows with a cool cloth or push back their hair from the forehead. Sometimes sensing a special need, she gave them a big hug.

64

＊

In this connection I think of the saintly Bishop Bienvenu in one of Victor Hugo's novels. Hugo writes of him, 'He understood how to sit down and hold his peace beside the man who had lost his wife, the mother who had lost her child. As he knew the moment for speech, he also knew the moment for silence.' He might have added, 'and the moment for touch'. In such hours when silence is called for, how much we can communicate through the medium of touch, through the clasp of a hand, or a hug. A friendly hand or an embrace can often be for others the very hand of God, the medium of divine comfort.

＊

One of the most moving articles I ever read, was based on a sermon preached by Dr William Sloane Coffin in the Riverside Church in New York, ten days after his son had died in a tragic accident in Boston harbour. In that sermon Dr Coffin gave some needed advice. 'The one thing which should never be said when a young person dies, is "It is the will of God." Never do we know enough to say that. In fact my consolation lies in knowing that it was not the will of God that Alec die, that when Alec drowned, God's was the first of all our hearts to break. Some of the very best of the healing flood of letters I received, and easily the worst, came from fellow-ministers, a few of whom proved they knew their Bibles better than the human condition. I know all the "right" Bible passages, including "Blessed are they that mourn". My faith is no house of cards; these passages are true, but the point is this, grief can render them unreal... That is why immediately after such a tragedy, people must come to your rescue, *people who only want to hold your hand*, not to quote anything, or even say anything, people who simply bring food and flowers – the basics of beauty and life – people who sign letters simply, "Your broken-hearted friend".'

＊

Donald Mackillop, a native of Harris, tells how, though the Western Isles culture in which he was brought up had much to commend it, it was not a tactile culture. Not until long after he had left Harris did he feel comfortable about holding his wife's hand in public. He went on to say that the few occasions when wives in Lewis and Harris would be seen publicly touching their husbands was to support them on their way home after a night's heavy drinking!

Verbal Banana-skins

Some misprints and Freudian slips may, like the foolishness of men, be the wisdom of God, but not always!

James McCready of Kilbirnie tells of a visit he paid to the Cathedral of the Isles in Millport. He noticed in the intimations, 'Today we welcome a sour preacher, Rev... ' He assumed this was supposed to read. 'We welcome as our preacher, Rev... '

❋

A minister's message in an American church newsletter was meant to read, 'Smile at someone who is hard to love. Say hello to someone who does not care much about you', but a misprint resulted in the second part appearing as, 'Say hell to someone who does not care much about you.'

❋

The church secretary was highly embarrassed when an office-bearer drew her attention to a misprint in the Sunday bulletin, 'While the minister is on holiday massages may be given to the church secretary.'

❋

A church bulletin issued an equally dubious invitation, 'Attend the monthly church dinner and you will hear an excellent speaker and heave a healthy meal.'

❋

In a church Order of Service, the line from the chorus of 'Onward Christian Soldiers', *'Christ the royal Master leads against the foe'* appeared as, *'Christ the royal master leans against the phone.'*

❋

A prayer given by a layman in the vestry before the morning service began with the words, 'Lord bless Thy servant as he leads our worship and eliminates the Gospel' – 'illuminates' was presumably what he meant to say!

❋

An American friend, Stephen Polley, told how he finally learned the colour of the wind! In the bulletin of a church in Pennsylvania, the printed call to worship read, 'We are listening for the sounds from Heaven. We hear the rush of a violet wind.'

❋

The Rev David Steele tells of joining worshippers one day in the printed Prayer of Affirmation. It began, 'We praise you God for the salt sea and the running water, for the eternal hiss, for the trees and the grass under our feet.' The eternal hiss! What surprised Dr Steele was that very few in the congregation seemed to think this strange. They just kept praying as though they had said nothing out of the ordinary. He wondered if they knew something about eternal hisses that he did not. He later learned that it should have read, 'eternal hills'!

✳

A John Clare from Durham tells how he can remember their vicar urging his congregation to remember those being persecuted in Communist Countries behind the Iron Curtain. He then proceeded to pray as earnestly as he could for Christians in 'Iron Country curtains'.

✳

When C. P. Scott, a life-long Unitarian, died, his close friend Bishop Barnes conducted his funeral service in Manchester Cathedral. In the course of his address the Bishop said, 'Scott like myself was a puzzled theist.' The reporter whom *The Times* had sent to cover the funeral was not into theological nuances. In his report for the following day's paper he wrote, 'The Bishop and Scott were puzzled atheists.'

✳

An interviewer on Ulster TV asked a passer-by, 'Do you think David Trimble will stick to his guns on disarmament?'

✳

When the boxer Mike Tyson was heavily defeated by Lennox Lewis, he said, 'It may be time for me to fade away into Bolivia.' I am not sure the Bolivian authorities would want Mike Tyson.

✳

Advertisement in a medical journal: 'Vacancies exist for two female physiotherapists. Varied work embracing in-patients and out-patients.'

✳

Seen in a newspaper under the heading 'Christmas greetings':

Adams Undertakers wish to thank all their clients and friends for the magnificent support they have received. We are looking forward to being of service to you next year.

❋

A Budget Car Hire website stated, '*Office hours are 24 hours, seven days a week. If you would like a rental car outwith these hours, we will be glad to assist. Just call the number below*.' That is what I call service.

❋

A lady who works in a travel agent tells how a typing error resulted in a Mr Savage being classified as a 'Brutish national'.

❋

In a magazine article I was once described as having a degree in 'unclear physics'.

❋

Some time ago the Memorial Awareness Board launched the Cemetery of the Year Award. With no hint of irony it announced that the 'deadline' for entries was the end of the month.

❋

The following correction appeared in the Althorne Village News; 'The recent article about the Ladies' Craft Club should have stated that Mrs Brown and Mrs Smith gave talks on "smocking and rugs respectively", not "smoking and drugs respectably".'

❋

Speaking of Nelson Mandela when he was elected President, Dame Jill Knight MP said, 'Anyone in his position needs to be whiter than white.'

❋

Commenting on the Arab-Israeli war, Warren Austin, the US delegate to the United Nations said, 'Let us all try to settle this problem like good Christians.'

❋

A television reporter told how Israeli troops had entered Hebron in search of the perpetrators of suicide bomb attacks.

❋

Dr Sandy Macdonald tells how during his year as Moderator of the General Assembly of the Church of Scotland, he was once introduced as the Generator of the Modern Church of Scotland.

❋

Shortly after the death of Princess Diana, football fans at Wembley were asked to pay silent tribute. At the end of the tribute, the radio commentator said, 'I have never heard a minute's silence like it.'

* * *

Most of us are guilty from time to time of such 'Foot In Mouth' howlers.

A woman was overheard saying to her friend, 'I seldom watch television. I turn it off more than I turn it on.' Another woman, who was partnering her husband in the golf club's mixed foursome, chipped the ball short of the green. Frustrated, she said, 'This green always looks closer than it is.' Her understanding husband, who had a knack of mixing up words, said, 'Don't feel bad. It is an obstacle illusion.'

* * *

A close friend of mine explained that the reason she had not been at the last dinner-dance, was that she had been indecapitated.

* * *

A worried mother said to her priest, 'It is as you often say, Father, "There is nothing but trouble in this transistory life".'

* * *

I think of a school where several classrooms were to be painted during the Easter holidays. The school having just received a new piano, the headmaster put a notice on top of it, 'Mind the piano.' You can guess what happened. The painter interpreted these words very differently. (In Scotland, 'mind' often means 'remember'.)

* * *

Kenneth McVicar tells how his elderly father preached one Sunday about Peter's denial of Jesus, and how after Peter had denied him the third time, the cock crew. That is what he meant to say but unfortunately said 'the corkscrew'. He tried to correct his mistake but still got it wrong. When the following Sunday he sought to apologise again, he still could not get it right.

* * *

A concerned church member waited behind to see her minister at the close of the service. 'My friend Mrs... is in real need. Could we possibly help her by using some of the discrepancy fund?' The minister decided not to embarrass her by drawing attention to her verbal faux pas. Instead he made the necessary sum available from his '*discretionary*' fund.

Pray for the Silence of...

Jeremy Paxman tells of an MP's maiden speech. Having delivered it, he retired exhausted and triumphant to the House of Commons tea room. There an elderly colleague complimented him with the words, 'That was a Rolls Royce of a speech.' It was however later pointed out to him that the old buffer said the same thing to almost every new MP, and that what he really meant was that it was well-oiled, almost inaudible and had gone on for a very long time.

❋

David Steel, the former leader of the Liberal Party, tells how as a young man he and other Presidents of University Unions were given wise advice on public speaking by Lord Birkett, one of the greatest orators of his day. 'First, you must emphasise the importance of the occasion. Second you must stress the weakness of the chosen vessel. Third, if time permits, you should turn to the subject.' I would be tempted to add a fourth piece of advice. Poke gentle fun at those present. Audiences enjoy the kindly wit of verbal cartoonists. There are few better examples of such wit than that which occurred at a dinner at which representatives of the army, navy and air force were the speakers. Proud of their traditions, the army and navy representatives both referred to the air force as the Cinderella of the forces. When it was the turn of the air force representative, he began, 'I know very little about Cinderella except that she had two ugly sisters.'

❋

Someone likened an after-dinner speech to a wheel – 'the longer the spoke, the greater the tire.'

> *Charm wit and brevity, may help one at the start*
> *But in the end it's brevity, that wins the public's heart.*

❋

There is nothing wrong with having nothing to say unless you insist on saying it.

❋

I listened recently to a speech which consisted of one joke after another. It was like being offered ice-cream all the time – after a while you hungered for something more substantial.

❋

A police constable and his wife were present at a dinner, at which, unknown to them, the main speaker was the Chief Constable. When he told one absolutely hilarious story, the guests burst into gales of laughter, all except the constable and his wife. They just sat with their hands on their knees, and a very disapproving look on their faces. When the man seated across the table said, 'Did you not think that was funny?' the constable replied, 'We cannot stand the man. We'll laugh at his joke when we go home.'

❋

Hecklers, especially those 'past the pint of no return', can present a problem. A speaker at a dinner in Glasgow posed the question, 'Where would we be without laughter?' He was momentarily speechless when a dinner guest shouted out, 'Edinburgh.'

❋

On rare occasions at dinners, it is the speaker who has had too much to drink. When a bride's father who had consumed not just his own wine but also the wine of the bridegroom's mother seated next to him, finally managed to get to his feet to propose the toast to the bride and groom, he launched into his opening joke. Getting the beginning wrong, he ploughed into ever deeper trouble. Finally to the great relief of his wife and many of the guests, he muttered, 'Oh to Hell. I never liked the joke anyway.'

❋

One evening when Churchill was addressing an audience in America, a gushing woman asked him, 'Does it not thrill you to know that every time you make a speech the hall is packed to overflowing?' 'It is flattering,' Churchill replied, 'but whenever I feel this way I always remember that if instead of making a political speech I was being hanged, the crowd would be twice as big.'

❋

A survey which I read recently said that the greatest fear of many people is speaking in public, and their second greatest fear is death. I would question that. I have never met anyone at a funeral who would rather be dead than paying the tribute.

❋

Accomplished speakers often make the art of after-dinner speaking appear easy. I think of the Rev James Currie, who spoke at more dinners and Burns Suppers in a year, than I have done in a lifetime. He had told his after-dinner stories so often that his timing was perfect.

On the few occasions when we both spoke at the same function, Jimmy would sit with pen poised ready to jot down any story or one-liner he had not heard before. He was so renowned for this, that in the after-dinner circuit he became known as 'the thief of bad gags'. On one occasion, noticing him writing furiously as I was speaking, I was tempted to turn and say, 'James, am I going slow enough for you?' My main criticism of those who at the beginning of a speech blatantly take out a pad and pen, is that they are not really listening to the speech for its own sake, but for the sake of their own next speech.

※

Whatever trouble Adam had
No man in days of yore
Could say when Adam cracked a joke
I've heard that one before.

※

I warm to the response of President Lyndon Johnson to an introduction he was once given: 'I wish my father and mother could have been here. My father would have enjoyed hearing it. My mother would have believed it.'

※

Occasionally at very formal dinners you are introduced by a specially hired Master of Ceremonies. Though immaculately attired in their red jackets, they don't always get things right. At a dinner at which Sir Leary Constantine, the West Indian cricketer, was the guest speaker, the red-jacketed MC instead of saying, 'Pray Silence for Sir Leary Constantine,' said, 'Pray for the Silence of Sir Leary Constantine.' Sir Leary slowly rose to his feet and said, 'Ladies and Gentlemen, your prayers have been answered,' and sat down. He did rise again a few seconds later.

※

At a WRI district dinner at which I was the guest speaker, the president began the evening by saying, 'Dr Simpson is our only speaker tonight. The rest of the evening will be entertainment.' I just hoped she never realised the implication of what she had said.

※

I remember once thanking a long-winded chairman for his gracious words of introduction. I said I could have listened to such an introduction all night. What I was then tempted to add was 'and for a few moments I thought I was going to have to'. But I refrained.

※

Another after-dinner speaker was not so tactful. Slowly rising to his feet after a very long and detailed introduction, he said that the only detail about him which the chairman had omitted was that he had been born by Caesarean section. Then he added, 'That explains why I like to leave houses by the window instead of the front door.'

※

On one occasion at a London dinner the chairman took 35 minutes to introduce the playwright George Bernard Shaw. After spending twenty minutes recounting the life history of Shaw, the chairman proceeded to give his own views on the subject which Shaw had been invited to address. When he finally said, 'I now call on George Bernard Shaw,' Shaw rose to his feet and said, 'Ladies and Gentlemen, the subject is not exhausted, but we are.' He then sat down and stayed seated.

※

I sometimes wonder why after-dinner speakers begin, 'Ladies and Gentlemen'. I am sure their audience all know who they are.

※

A judge used the language of the law-courts to shed light on the art of after-dinner speaking. 'You must have an *arresting* beginning, a few appropriate *sentences* for the middle, and a *brief* ending. You must also speak with *conviction*.' But in fact more is needed than that. I recall speaking at a Glasgow dinner at which the Governor of the Bank of England was the other speaker. He spoke for half an hour on the state of the economy. The problem is that most people don't come to a dinner to be educated, let alone bored. They come to be entertained, to exercise what Ken Dodd called their 'chuckle muscles.' It was because laughter is a helpful aid to digestion, that our ancestors arranged for jesters to be present at banquets. I sometimes wonder if after dinner speakers are their modern equivalent?

※

At the Yalta conference after President Roosevelt offered a flowery toast to Stalin as a lover of peace, the Soviets awaited a toast by Churchill. Churchill growled in a whisper to a member of his staff, 'But Stalin does not want peace.' But after urging from the staff member, he rose and said, 'A toast to Premier Stalin, whose conduct of foreign policy manifests a desire for peace.' As he sat down he muttered, 'A piece of Poland, a piece of Czechoslovakia, a piece of Romania...'

Formative Influences

Many today tend to think of the individual in isolation, with only incidental reference to others. A person is imagined as being the sum of his or her individual ideas, passions, strengths and weaknesses. Such a person is viewed as living in imaginary solitariness, rather than in relationship, but in fact our personality is shaped by our relationships with other people, especially those we admire. These relationships are not something added on to a fundamentally private self. They have in fact made us the people we are. At various stages in my life different people have impacted on me. *Let me profile a few of the more famous ones.*

Fanny Blankers Koen and John Charles

The publicity surrounding the deaths early in 2004 of Fanny Blankers Koen, the most outstanding woman athlete of the 20th century, and John Charles, one of soccer's all-time greats, conjured up fond boyhood memories. What wonderful role models they were for young people of my generation. In his long and distinguished career, Charles was never once yellow or red-carded. Fanny Blankers Koen first competed in the 1936 Berlin Olympics. For the teenage Blankers Koen, the highlight of these Games was getting the autograph of Jesse Owens, the black American sprinter who by winning four gold medals shattered Hitler's dream of proving to the world that the Germans were the Master Race. Twelve years later in the London Olympics, Fanny herself won four gold medals – in the sprints, the hurdles and the relay. One can only surmise how many more Olympic medals Blankers Koen might have won, had the war not cancelled the 1940 and 1944 Games, or if Olympic rules had allowed her to contest more than four events, for she was also the world record holder in the high jump, long jump, and the 800m. The latter event was not included in the '48 Olympics because medical opinion then believed that women who competed over such long distances 'would become old too soon'! I wonder what Paula Radcliffe would make of that!

Fanny Blankers Koen was stunningly modest. When she and Jesse Owens met as honoured spectators at the 1972 Olympics, she said, 'I still have your autograph. I am Fanny Blankers Koen.' 'You don't have to tell me,' he said, 'I know everything about you.' Recounting this later, she said, 'How amazing that Jesse Owens should know who I was.'

Speaking shortly before her death about her athletic career, she said, 'It was very different then – no money, but no drugs either. Overall I think we had more fun than athletes do now.' Likewise there was no trace of envy in John Charles. Before the onset of Alzheimer's disease, the gentle Welsh giant delivered his verdict on today's soccer millionaires: 'There is not as much fun in the game today. It is all about money.' The clamour for victory is so deafening that in the world of professional sport the voice of noble ideals can scarcely get a hearing. We are more likely to find evidence to confirm such clichés as, 'the winner takes all', 'few befriend losers' and 'money speaks all languages'. Few players or supporters today cherish such maxims as 'the game for the game's sake' (the motto of Queen's Park football club), or 'may the best team win'.

In our fiercely competitive culture, we need role models of the stature of Blankers Koen and John Charles.

Albert Schweitzer and Toyohiko Kagawa

During the final years of my secondary education, Robert Thomson, our English teacher, introduced us to some of the truly great lives of the early 20th century. Knowing how important heroes are in the lives of young people, he encouraged us to read the biographies of Edward Wilson of the Antarctic, Toyohiko Kagawa – the Japanese saint who devoted his life to improving the lot of the slum dwellers in Tokyo – and Albert Schweitzer – who gave up a celebrity lifestyle and a university professorship to study medicine, in order to go to West Africa 'to try and repay a little of the debt the white man owed to the black man'. Aware that we were constantly bombarded by mostly negative role models, Mr Thomson sought to give us some positive ones. As he probably suspected, I personally was challenged by the incredible courage of Edward Wilson, the compassion and humility of Toyohiko Kagawa, and the intellect and passion of Albert Schweitzer.

As a young man Kagawa read how 'Jesus went about doing good'. He said he found that very disconcerting, for up until then he had been content with just going about. Countless are the moving stories about Toyohiko Kagawa. One will suffice. Prior to the start of a large convention at which he was to be the guest speaker, Toyohiko and some of the other officials adjourned to the toilet. As often happens, many of the men missed the wastepaper baskets with their discarded paper towels. When the other platform guests made to return to the top table, they assumed Dr Kagawa was right behind them. But on turning round, he was nowhere to be seen. He was finally located in the toilet gathering up the towels that others had left for the cleaners to pick up.

In my Higher English exam, we had to write an essay on one of several suggested titles. Opting for 'the doctor' I proceeded to write about Schweitzer. In the afternoon literature paper, one question concerned a biography that had made an impact on us. I chose George Seaver's biography of Albert Schweitzer! I just hoped it would be a different marker for the second paper. Schweitzer certainly helped me pass my final school exams. But his influence on me was much greater than that. He reminded me that true greatness is measured by service.

One of my favourite stories about Schweitzer, who was later awarded the Nobel Peace Prize, tells how he was working one day in the boiling heat of the West African sun, putting the finishing touches to the roof of his new hospital in Lambarene. Calling over to a relative of one of his patients, a man sitting in the shade of a nearby tree, Schweitzer said, 'Would you care to give me a hand?' 'I am sorry,' said the African, 'I don't do manual work. You see, I am an intellectual.' On hearing this, Dr Schweitzer, who was a doctor of philosophy, a doctor of theology, a doctor of music and a doctor of medicine, replied, 'I once tried to be an intellectual too, but I could not live up to it.'

Professor Fred Craddock tells an equally moving story about Schweitzer. While a divinity student he wrote a lengthy essay critical of Dr Schweitzer's unorthodox interpretation of the New Testament. For the essay he was awarded an A Grade. Shortly after writing it, he happened to read how the elderly Dr Schweitzer was coming to Cleveland to give a recital on a new church organ, and afterwards to meet informally with the audience. In preparation for this encounter Fred re-read his essay and Dr Schweitzer's controversial book, *The Quest for the Historical Jesus*. He would challenge Dr Schweitzer's right to call himself a Christian. When the recital finished, he rushed downstairs to the fellowship hall, grabbed a biscuit and coffee and sat down on one of the front seats. Finally Dr Schweitzer came in. He was about 75. His hair was white and long, his moustache bushy. Fred was ready with his theological questions. When Dr Schweitzer rose to speak, he said, 'Can I thank you for your generous reception of me, and your considerable contribution to my African hospital. Next week I will be returning there, for my people are sick and hungry and many are dying. How I wish that some of you who have in you the love

76

of Jesus would come and help me.' On hearing that, Fred stuffed the theological questions he had jotted down into his pocket and quietly left the hall, beating his breast with shame.

William Barclay

Although some people think that the term 'light-hearted Christian' is an oxymoron, rather like 'random order', and 'farewell reception', the Christians who exerted the greatest influence on me all practised a religion that had a deep and joyous laugh in it. I think especially of two of my teachers, Professors William Barclay and Reinhold Niebuhr. Both men had a lively sense of humour. They both took God seriously, but not themselves. They were for me living proof that exceptionally gifted, gracious and large-hearted people can be deeply humble, and that reverence and humour can go hand in hand. They were also models of life-enhancing faith. They both fulfilled what Dr Barclay once said was the true test of religion: 'Does it make wings to lift people up, or is it a dead weight to drag them down? Does it make for joy or depression? Are people haunted or helped by it? Does it carry you, or do you have to carry it?'

Long before Dr Barclay taught me New Testament studies, he had been chaplain to the secondary school I attended. He later officiated at my wedding. It was Dr Barclay who first encouraged me to write. He felt my scientific and Biblical training, my love of illustration and sense of humour, could make the Gospel live for those seldom inside a church. He himself was one of the finest communicators and premier storytellers of the 20th century, the modern equivalent of the Jewish Talmudic scholars, who more than two thousand years before had developed and embellished the art of interpretation, analogy and painting memorable word pictures.

Though Dr Barclay was ungainly of build, very deaf, and had a rather harsh-sounding voice, there was such a dynamic quality about his broadcasting that people from all walks of life tuned in to his radio and television broadcasts. When a Glasgow lady was asked, as part of a BBC survey, about her favourite television programmes, she replied, '*This is Your Life*, and that deaf old man who talks about the Bible'!

Dr Barclay loved to tell the story of a four-year-old girl who was sitting on the front wall of her house enjoying a huge lollipop. She was sticky from ear to ear. Along the road came her five-year-old boy-friend. 'Give me a sook at your lolly,' he said. 'No,' she said, 'but when I am finished and all sticky, I will let you kiss me.' Dr Barclay said he often wished he could have said 'No' as politely as that. It would certainly have lightened his immense workload. As well as his lecturing and speaking commitments he would often write three books in a year.

His daughter Barbara and I attended Eastwood Secondary School. At the age of nineteen she accompanied her boy-friend and his parents to Northern Ireland for a sailing holiday. Dr Barclay was at the time occupying the pulpit in one of Edinburgh's West End churches. When he was informed on the Saturday that Barbara was missing, feared drowned, he immediately flew to Northern Ireland. A week later, her body and her boy-friend's body had still not been found. Returning to Scotland he told the packed congregation that he was going to preach the sermon he had planned to preach the previous Sunday. He had two texts, 'Moses drew near to the thick darkness' and 'Jesus said, I am the light of the world'. The silence in the church was palpable.

I had the privilege of being present when Dr Barclay recorded his last television lecture. When he was about five minutes into the recording, I noticed him moving several pages of his manuscript. When the recording finished, James Dey, the BBC producer, told us that he had just witnessed one of the most amazing happenings in his career in broadcasting. A few minutes into the recording Dr Barclay realised he had the wrong manuscript. Most broadcasters, he said, would have either stopped and started again, or they would have finished before the allotted time, or exceeded it. But Dr Barclay finished right on time. In his reply Dr Barclay said it was strange his broadcasting career should end in this way, for it had begun many years before in Williamwood Church in similar fashion. During his first live broadcast on what was then the Light Programme, with an audience of millions, the sleeve of his gown caused his manuscript to fall from the pulpit. He delivered the rest of his sermon without notes, again within the allotted time. I sometimes doubt if we shall see his like again.

In the field of theology my amateur standing has never been questioned! Whatever communication skills I have lie in being able to speak to what Dr Barclay called 'the plain man', to interpret the gospel in phrases and stories that arrest the mind and hopefully also arouse the imagination. That art I learned from William Barclay more than anyone else.

Reinhold Niebuhr

For a year I had the immense privilege of studying in New York, and meeting there one of the most monumental minds of the 20th century. Reinhold Niebuhr had such a brilliant mind that he could have attained eminence in any field. He had been President Franklin Roosevelt's adviser. He was a close friend of the poet Auden. Though a stroke had left his speech slightly indistinct, and one arm less than fully functional, the breadth of his knowledge, and the profundity of his insights and the sharpness of his wit made a deep impression. I sat transfixed in his class on the Ethics of International Relations. There seemed to be no phase of human history, and no aspect of politics, that he did not have at his fingertips. I recall him telling us that 'our causes are never as righteous as we think they are, and our participation in them is never as free of self-interest as we claim', and that 'the children of darkness are sometimes not only wiser but often more appealing and plausible than the children of light'. 'The worst evil is often done, not by obviously evil people, but by *righteous* people who do not know the limits of their righteousness'. That, he said, 'is the essence of sin'. He spoke of there being a very real place for humour 'in the outer courts of the temple, and for its echo being heard in the sanctuary'. He spoke of little children indulging freely in a laughter 'which expressed the pure animal joy of existence'. He hoped this sense of humour would develop so that they would be able to laugh at themselves.

During the debate on Iraq at the 2003 Assembly of the Church of Scotland, I recalled how in his book *The Irony of American History*, published in 1952, Dr Niebuhr had predicted that the 'winner' of the cold war would inevitably 'face the imperial problem of using power in global terms, but from one particular centre of authority, so dominant and unchallenged that its world rule would almost certainly violate basic standards of justice'. He went on to warn that if America became that dominant nation, it would not recognise its own injustices toward others, 'for our good intentions in world affairs would be so self-evident to us. We find it almost as difficult as the communists to believe that anyone could think ill of us, since we are as persuaded as the communists that our society is so essentially virtuous that only malice could prompt criticism of any of our actions.' What interest that quotation roused in the Assembly. Though some of what Reinhold Niebuhr taught me remains with me, it was the man who left the deeper mark.

Charles Malik

The most memorable visiting lecturer during my year at Union Seminary in New York was Charles Malik, the President of the United Nations General Assembly. His address made such an impression on many of us that he was approached to allow it to be printed. Let me share a few sentences: 'There is truth and there is falsehood. There is good and there is evil. There is happiness and there is misery. There is freedom and there is slavery. There is that which ennobles and there is that which demeans. There is that which conduces to strength and health, and there is that which conspires to weakness and disease... There is that which puts you in harmony with yourself, with others, with the universe, with God, and there is that which alienates you from yourself, from the world and from God... Should you read the Bible, especially the Psalms and the Gospels reverently and prayerfully; should you read the writings of the deepest and purest saints of God; should you faithfully serve the church and participate in the fullness of its life, despite its endless frailties and imperfections and tribulations; should you practise the great art of mental and moral discipline; should you seek with love and expectation the company of those who do those things, I guarantee you two things: first you will experience in your own life and being a taste of what is beautiful and strong and certain and free; and second you will develop such a sharpness of vision as to distinguish the true from the false whenever you come across them.'

George Webber and William Stringfellow

During my stay in Manhattan I visited the East Harlem Protestant Parish on the East Side of the City. At that time a group of very dedicated people, led by the Rev George Webber and a lawyer, William Stringfellow, were working in the notorious Harlem district. They, and the other members of the Community which they had founded, tried among other things to find jobs for blacks and Puerto Ricans, many of whom because of the language barrier, or drug or alcohol problems, or lack of any kind of training, were virtually unemployable. I came away full of admiration for their determination to do what they could to try and improve the living conditions of the black people of Harlem, and counteract the gang culture. William Stringfellow told how one summer there were eleven homicides as a result of gang warfare. Two gangs, one Italian and one Puerto Rican, were engaged in vicious territorial disputes.

One of the issues at stake was which gang had jurisdiction over a public swimming pool in a neighbourhood where the heat and the humidity soared in the summer. In the fight between these two particular gangs, the brother of one of the war counsellors was killed. In gang society in the late 1950s, the war counsellor was the gang leader. On the night of the fight, the brother of the boy who had been killed spent a long time brooding over his immense loss, and the meaning of death. Finally he decided to visit his counterpart in the rival gang, his mortal enemy. He went alone, without bodyguards or weapons. They talked of what had happened and what it meant to those still living. After a while a council was formed to discuss and negotiate the differences between the two gangs. Several radical changes resulted from that meeting. After the council was formed there was no further serious physical violence. They also decided to invite one of the local policemen to sit down with them and say whatever he had to say. This was the first time these kids had confronted a policeman in any situation except one of hostility and suspicion. It was the familiar story, 'By the death of one many were reconciled.' It was that story which later became the basis for Leonard Bernstein's musical *West Side Story*.

Tom Cousins

In a letter concerning my visit to Columbia Seminary in Atlanta in 1995, Dr Oldenburg, the President of the College, inquired whether during my stay, I would like to play Augusta National, that spectacularly beautiful golf course in Georgia where the 'Masters' is played every year. Instead of writing back, I faxed immediately, intimating my willingness to accept!

For me, every bit as memorable as flying by private jet to Augusta, and playing Augusta National, was getting to know my pilot and host: Tom Cousins, the Chief Executive of Cousins Properties, the firm which had built many of the prominent Atlanta landmarks. Tom is not only a very fine golfer and committed churchman, he is also one of America's greatest philanthropists. Whereas some very wealthy people, by their aloofness, make everyone else feel small, Tom makes everyone he meets feel important. I instinctively warmed to him. The year before my visit, Tom had chosen a golf course as the unlikely centrepiece for one of the great social experiments of the late 20th century, the reviving of the run-down, crime-and-drug-ridden neighbourhood of East Lake in Atlanta. Shortly after the

Ryder Cup was hosted at East Lake Country Club in 1963, resulting in a runaway victory for the American team captained by Arnold Palmer, the golf course, and the surrounding area, became more and more run-down. Partly as a tribute to Bobby Jones, who as a boy and young man had learned his golf at East Lake, Tom Cousins decided to purchase the course and clubhouse and set about restoring it to the original design of the Scottish golf architect, Donald Ross. The fairways and greens were returfed. The lake became once again the dominant feature of the course. The Georgian clubhouse, which like everything else about the area had been neglected, was restored to its original splendour. The cart-paths were removed, for it concerned Tom that many Americans, when not sitting at their office desk, were seated either in their car, or in an armchair watching television, or on a golf cart. He wanted the East Lake members to do more driving with a club than a cart.

A remark by a criminal justice professor, that if you improve the quality of life in a neighbourhood, you have a better chance of reducing crime, inspired Tom to try and rehabilitate what had become one of Atlanta's most blighted areas, in fact such a war zone that it was often referred to as 'Little Vietnam'. He hoped that by improving the housing and work prospects of the local residents, the majority of whom were living on welfare, he could breathe new life into the East Lake community.

One of the first things he did was to employ local youths as caddies, with the promise of college scholarships for those showing diligence and potential. (The day I played the East Lake golf course with my son, both our caddies were proud winners of such scholarships.) To further his social dream, Tom sought the support of friends who were big names in the golfing world, such as Tiger Woods and Jack Nicklaus. He also signed up 82 companies as corporate members, including Coca-Cola, Xerox and AT&T. Each corporate membership cost $275,000, of which $200,000 was spent revitalising the surrounding neighbourhood.

Whereas the local people might have questioned the motives of other wealthy businessmen, the majority of the East Lake residents trusted Tom. They were certain that what he was proposing was not an attempt to line his own pockets, but was genuinely for their benefit. Four hundred acres of poor quality housing and very few public amenities were transformed into one of the most impressive mixed-income communities in America. But more than that, Tom provided for the residents public amenities such as a large swimming pool, tennis courts, an elementary school, a YMCA and a public golf course, named after one of Tom's close friends in Atlanta, Charlie Yates, a former Amateur champion. As Jack Nicklaus said, 'What Tom has done in East Lake is unbelievable.' A few years ago, Tom was presented with the Bobby Jones award for his immense contribution to the game of golf. There have been few if any worthier winners.

Tom has long regarded his wealth as a sacred trust to be used to enrich the lives of others. What Tom has achieved in Atlanta stemmed, as someone said, from his 'deeply held, but not advertised Christian belief, that from him to whom much is given, much shall be required.' It is the deep faith of Tom and his wife Anne that fuels their philanthropic work.

Cardinal Hume and Jonathan Sacks

The Presbyterian Church lives by the philosophy that the person 'whose term of office is short, little harm can do'. Moderators of the General Assembly of the Church of Scotland are consequently elected for only one year. Being Moderator is an immense privilege, for during your year in office you represent the Church at home and abroad. My year in office – 1994–1995, was the year of several significant 50th anniversaries. It began in June with the 50th-anniversary open-air service in Portsmouth to commemorate probably the most dramatic military operation in all history – the D-Day invasion – and it ended with the 50th-anniversary service in St Paul's Cathedral in London to commemorate VE day.

The Portsmouth Service was attended by the Queen, Prime Minister John Major, President Bill Clinton, and dignitaries from more than forty countries. More important still, it was attended by hundreds of veterans who had taken part in the D-Day invasion. The latter were cheered as they walked the streets that day. The weather for the service was perfect, unlike the torrential downpours of the previous day. As we drove in procession to the arena, my wife Helen said, 'I know you are to be sitting between Archbishop Carey and Cardinal Hume. Where do you think I will be seated?' With a deadpan face, I said, 'Probably between Mrs Carey and Mrs Hume.' 'I know Eileen Carey,' Helen replied, 'but what is Mrs Hume like?' 'Helen,' I said, 'if the wife of the Cardinal appears today, there will be little mention tomorrow of D-Day in the tabloid newspapers!' How we laughed. Being just a ten-year-old schoolboy when D-Day took place, I was thrilled fifty years later to be able to catch a few echoes of the actual event and meet some of the brave men who took part.

Later that year, during my visit as Moderator to London, I had the honour of spending time with Cardinal Hume in his London home. In an age which focuses on questionable celebrities, he was living proof that humility and genuine spirituality still have a power and presence of their own. In his company you felt your mind and spirit being enlarged. When at the end of my visit, I presented him with a copy of my book *All About Christmas*, he in return gave me a signed copy of one of his books, asking me to forgive the pretentiousness of the title, *Remaking Europe*. 'The title was chosen by the publisher, certainly not by me.'

During that same visit I also had the privilege of visiting Britain's Chief Rabbi in his London home. Having got through the elaborate security system, I was greeted by a very friendly man with a warm smile. Dr Jonathan Sacks is one of those people who, when he speaks of God in our secular age, is listened to. He is an outstanding thinker, respected not only by academics, but by those of a less academic bent. In the introduction to his simple, yet profound book *Celebrating Life*, he tells how his mother had kept asking him to write a book she could understand. 'This book,' he said, 'is my response to her request.' I enjoyed Dr Sacks' sense of humour. When asked on one occasion who the formative influences were in his life, he replied, 'My late father, who was always prepared to lose a friend rather than compromise a principle, and my mother who kept all the friends my father lost.'

In his classic *The Dignity of Difference*, Dr Sacks expresses his deep longing that dialogue between those of different faiths should replace disputation, that each faith should search for a way of living with and acknowledging the integrity of those who are not of their faith. Expounding this theme in *The Times*, he told how there were once two men who spent their lives transporting stones. One carried rocks, the other diamonds. One day they were given emeralds to carry. The man who had spent his days carrying rocks saw emeralds as just another burden of no intrinsic value. The one who regularly carried diamonds recognised emeralds as another form of precious stone, different, but with their own distinctive beauty. Then Dr Sacks added, 'So it is with faith. If your own faith is nothing more than a burden, you will not value the faith of others. But if you cherish your faith, you will value other people's faith also, even though it is different from your own. You will know that faiths are like jewels. One is especially your own, but all are precious.'

Ding-a-Ling-Ling

Father Deeny tells how an eight-year-old boy faithfully turned up each Sunday for early Mass. He came early to help prepare the elements. At the solemn moment of consecration of the bread and the wine, he would ring some handbells. One Sunday when the moment of consecration arrived, the boy suddenly realised that he had left the handbells in the vestry. Using his initiative he shouted in a loud voice, 'Ding-a-ling-ling.'

❋

Few minds have been more alert to the ludicrous and the incongruous than that of the Rev Sydney Smith. Speaking one day of his brother, who was a famous lawyer, he said, 'My brother rose by way of gravity and I sank by way of levity.'

❋

Bishop Sheen told how a letter addressed to Lord God Almighty was forwarded to him by the postmaster in Washington DC. It asked God to send $50 immediately. Sheen told how he finally decided to send $25 so that the man would not lose faith in God. A week later the postmaster forwarded another letter to Bishop Sheen addressed in the same way by the same man. It again asked for $50. This letter had however a P.S., 'This time Lord, send the money through Cardinal Spellman of New York, because last time Bishop Sheen held back $25.'

❋

A Bishop is reported to have declined an invitation to say Grace at a certain dinner. He explained that he did not want God to know he was going to be present.

❋

Next to a city church was a popular restaurant. Its kitchen equipment was evidently needing attention, for one day the local doctor noticed, parked outside the church, a mechanic's truck with a sign, 'Refrigerated services'. Being a committed churchman, he hoped nobody would think the sign referred to the Sunday services. Did he perhaps recall what Robert Burns wrote about a visit to the church at Lamington?

> *As cauld a wind as ever blew*
> *A cauld kirk and in't but few*
> *As cauld a minister as ever spak*
> *It will be long ere I'll be back.*

General Wolfe expressed much the same sentiment in a letter to his mother, during his stay in Glasgow in 1749. 'I do several things as

Commanding Officer which I would never think of doing otherwise. For instance I'm at the Kirk every Sunday... ' Then he added: 'The generality of Scottish preachers are excessive blockheads, so truly and obstinately dull... '

Included in the 250th anniversary booklet of Trinity Episcopal Church in Staunton, Virginia, is a story about how a seven-year-old suddenly exclaimed to his Sunday School teacher, 'Can we hurry up. This is boring.' Immediately the little girl next to him gave him a dig in the ribs. 'Be quiet,' she said. 'It is supposed to be boring.' It saddens me when I hear of grown-ups also being put off the church because of boring, refrigerated services, for joyful, meaningful worship is I believe one of the best antidotes to the secularism, materialism and selfish individualism which so disfigure life today. Hymns ought not to be sung as dirges. Worship, as Bishop Tutu said, can be fun.

✳

A blank square appeared in the newsletter of a church. Below it were these words: 'Blow on the square. If it turns green, call your doctor. If it turns brown call your dentist. If it turns purple, see your psychiatrist. If it turns black, call your lawyer and check your will. If it remains the same colour there is no reason why you should not be in church this Sunday!'

✳

A Scottish newspaper (*The Herald*) carried the story of a Scottish pound note which met a £20 note in a man's wallet. (We still have pound notes in Scotland.) 'Where have you been?' asked the pound note. 'Oh, pretty nearly everywhere,' said the twenty-pound note. 'A day at the races, posh bars, lots of nights out — what about yourself?' 'Oh, just the usual,' said the pound note: 'Church, church, church.'

I warm to the minister's original offertory prayer, 'O Lord why is it that a ten-pound note looks so large in the offering plate and so small in the supermarket?' 'I cannot stand change,' said another minister, 'especially in the collection.' How often the church's financial problems stem from the fact that many of her members give weakly rather than weekly.

✳

Sheepdog trials are fascinating to watch, the dog responding to the great variety of the shepherd's whistles. In the Highlands, sheepdogs were almost always at the shepherd's side. In the 19th century they even accompanied them to church. When sheepdogs are mentioned I often recall a story which Dr George Johnstone Jeffrey told. He was a man of great good will and wit. On one occasion he had spoken to a group of country children about the 23rd Psalm – 'The Lord is my shepherd' – a psalm greatly revered in Scotland. He asked the children what they thought of it. 'Not much,' said one little girl. 'It is all about a shepherd and it never mentions his dog.' 'I wonder if you are right,' said Dr Jeffrey. 'Let us read it through together. When they came to the last verse, '*Goodness* and *Mercy* all my life shall surely follow me,' Dr Jeffrey said, 'There you have the names of not just one dog but two, accompanying the shepherd.'

✳

American visitors to Scotland often marvel at our harvest thanksgiving services. We go in for them in such a big way, decorating the church, not just with a chaste bowl of flowers, but piling the fruits of the farm, the field and garden in the chancel and at the doors. What a lovely fragrance. And the singing! Suburban businessmen and women who have ploughed up nothing, except perhaps the golf course, expand their lungs to proclaim, 'We plough the fields and scatter, the good seed on the land', or the more modern version, 'We plough the fields with tractors, with drills we sow the land'.

✳

Dr Archie Craig, one of the Church's outstanding Moderators, had a wonderful sense of humour. He chuckled as he told of the psychiatrist who looked immensely stressed. Asked by a colleague if he was all right, he replied, 'No. I need to see a psychiatrist.' 'But you *are* a psychiatrist,' protested the other. 'I know, but I charge too much.' Dr Craig also loved to recount how, in notes he had prepared for an address to a Temperance Rally in the old St Andrews Hall in Glasgow, he discovered that towards the end of his address he had typed, 'And now two final pints.' On another occasion, he told with great gusto how in the corner of a railway carriage, there sat an exquisite young man – a tailor's dream of a young man – with the latest model of bowler hat, a suit cut to perfection, and an umbrella rolled to an unbelievable slimness. One manicured hand rested elegantly on the umbrella handle, while the other toyed daintily with a new pair of doeskin gloves. From diagonally opposite, a small girl gazed at him unflinchingly, before asking in a piercing voice, 'Mummy, what is that funny man for?'

✳

Professor David Fergusson of Edinburgh University tells how the old system of University faculties and departments was recently abolished and replaced by a new system of schools and colleges. The Faculty of Divinity was merged with five other faculties in a single academic division, including Law, Education, Social Sciences, Arts and Music. When the Principal of the University was asked what these faculties had in common to justify a single academic division, he used a phrase from the 18th-century Scottish Enlightenment: 'You are all united in your common pursuit of the science of man.' In the light of that explanation, it was humorously suggested that the new division might be renamed 'Man United'!

❋

An elderly American lady told her daughter, as they made their way out of church, 'Quit griping about your church. If it was perfect you could not belong.'

❋

Towards the end of the millennium a minister was asked if he would speak to a gathering of church office-bearers about preparing for the 21st century. The minister quipped that his problem was that some of his own office-bearers were still preparing for the 20th.

❋

Mary Slessor, the mill girl from Dundee who exerted such an influence for good on the people of Calabar in Africa, is my idea of a real saint. I love her honesty. Having read some of the things Paul had written about women, she was heard to say, 'Now, now laddie, this will not do.' On another occasion, at the end of a very tiring day, she threw herself on her bed, saying, 'Father, I am too tired to say my prayers. You say them for me.'

❋

A final year divinity student was asked to conduct the Remembrance Day service. Suffering from lack of inspiration she approached her tutor for some guidance. 'I'm finding this one a problem,' she said. 'What can I possibly say about the two world wars? After all, I wasn't born until 1970.' Her tutor was silent for a moment but then said, 'You are going to have a real problem come Christmas, aren't you?'

❋

A cartoon depicted Mary and Joseph arriving at the Bethlehem inn. Above the inn, the star is shining brightly. Mary is saying to Joseph, 'There is no way I am going to stay in a one-star hotel.'

❋

When a minister asked the children why Mary and Joseph took the boy Jesus with them to Jerusalem, one of them replied, 'Maybe they couldn't get a baby-sitter.'

❋

A small girl interpreted the opening words of Handel's *Messiah*, 'Comfort Ye, Comfort Ye', to mean: 'Come for tea, come for tea...'

The programme for a carol concert intimated one of the readings as 'The Shepherds go to the Manager'. Did they feel they were being fleeced, or was their intention to negotiate a pay rise?

✻

An American minister tells how one of their family dolls looked so like a real baby, that it was used year after year as the baby Jesus in the church nativity play. When the minister's son was four, he told his Sunday school teacher, 'We keep Jesus in the closet and bring him out every Christmas.' How many adults do just that. At Christmas we acknowledge and carol Jesus as Lord, but throughout the year take our bearings from our contemporaries — from the lights of passing ships rather than the stars.

✻

'What would have happened had it been Three Wise Women rather than Three Wise Men who had journeyed to Bethlehem?' To that hypothetical question, one woman answered, 'They would have arrived on time, cleaned the stable, helped with the delivery of the baby, made a casserole and brought practical gifts.'

✻

One Christmas, the autocratic Earl of Yarborough prefaced his reading of Luke's account of the shepherds leaving their flocks to go and see the babe in Bethlehem, with the remark, 'I'd like to say before reading this lesson that if they had been my shepherds I would have sacked them.'

✻

Lord David Steel recalls how, when he fought his first General Election as Liberal leader in 1979, word reached him of the preparations in one of London's fashionable churches for the Sunday service following the election. The vicar told the organist that if the Conservatives won, they would open with the hymn, *Now thank we all our God*, and if Labour won they would begin with, *Oh God our help in ages past*. The organist, who was secretary of the local Liberal association, asked the vicar what he would do if the Liberals won. 'In that case,' replied the vicar, 'we'll have *God moves in a mysterious way*.'

✻

Someone once said that the Church of England had the engine of a lawn-mower and the brakes of a juggernaut. That applies to more than the C of E. One of the numerous light-bulb jokes concerns the Presbyterian Church. 'How many Presbyterians does it take to change a light bulb? The answer is one, but nine others will tell you they preferred the old one.' The Status Quo committee is the one committee that the Church has not thought to invent, perhaps because those who would be the ideal candidates for membership are fully occupied on all the other committees.

✻

Dr Fred Craddock tells of seeing in a churchyard a grave at right angles to all the others. It took up three burial plots. As he contemplated this anomaly, a man who was passing said, 'I knew the deceased. We were in the same church. When he died his family asked if he could be buried at an angle, for he was always at cross purposes with everyone else. He was never pleased with anything at home or church. "Why did they ask him to do that?" "Who gave him authority?" "They should have chosen Mr X not Mr Y." He said that kind of thing the whole time. The family decided not to try and change him just because he was dead. So they buried him crosswise.' I suspect there are in every congregation one or two members who should be similarly buried?

✻

Richard Lischer, in his book *Open Secrets* says, 'One part of the church goes to great expense in order to prepare a theologian for another part of the church that really wants a guitar player.'

✻

Parents must sometimes wish their children could skip the 'I do it myself' stage – that stage when two-year-old Natalie insists on pouring milk over her *Cheerios* even though she lacks the dexterity to stop when the bowl is full, or when she puts her wellingtons on the wrong feet. Many children as they approach adolescence unfortunately 'progress' to a stage when they are willing to do only those things at which they excel. I wonder if one of the 'child-like' qualities which Jesus admired was that which reflects a willingness to have a go. Community and church life would be enriched if, when volunteers are needed, more ordinary folk were willing to say, 'I will do it myself.' Some of the best Sunday school teachers I have known have not been experts in the history or geography of Palestine. Some of the best youth workers have been those who have had a deep concern for young people. This often compensated for their lack of professional qualifications. God continues to be pretty good at using the efforts of one-talented people.

✻

Dr Archie Craig once heard an aged C of S minister pray '*that the grand old institution of the Scottish Sabbath may never be secularised, continentalised, paganised or Anglicanised.*'

During an exercise class at a large American church one woman participant refused to try and touch her toes: 'If God had wanted me to touch my toes, he would have put them on my knees!'

The Rev Charles Partee tells how after conducting worship for a month in his first charge, his senior elder took him aside and said, 'We think we are going to like you a lot, but your sermons are going right over our heads. Remember that Jesus said, "Feed my sheep", not my giraffes.' Numerous other not very complimentary things have been said about ministers' sermons:

'His "lastly" was a consummation devoutly to be wished.'

'If his text had had scarlet fever, his sermon would not have caught it.'

'His text would have fitted any sermon, and the sermon would have fitted any text.'

'He was a walking and talking anaesthetic.'

A golfer apologised to his companions for being late one Sunday morning: 'I flipped a coin to decide whether to play golf or go to church. I had to flip it fifteen times.'

Some of the best story-writing is done by the 'What if' method. Dr Ernest Campbell suggests a few what-ifs for the Bible and the Church:

1. What if Moses and his friends had found Egyptian culture user-friendly and settled in?

2. What if Samson had gone to a different barber?

3. What if the returning prodigal had met his elder brother first?

4. What if Judas had not gone for the money? Would there be five gospels instead of four?

We could add some more:

5. What if Noah, waiting for the dove to return, had received not an olive leaf, but a note saying, 'Jews not wanted on Mt Ararat. Go find your own mountain.' Would Noah and his family have become the world's first boat people?

6. What if Paul had been married? Would he have said what he did about women?

7. What if Adam and Eve, when they decided to sew clothing for themselves, had mistakenly used poison ivy instead of fig leaves?

Dornoch Memories

Dornoch is a unique little town, situated on the North Sea, 45 miles north of Inverness. Its charm might possibly be lost to the world at large, were it not for three great assets — its world famous golf course, described by a leading golf-writer as 'A Dream by a Scottish Shore', its attractive mediaeval cathedral where I was minister for many years, and the glory of its beaches and surrounding countryside. I have a love affair with all three.

❄

The 13th-century Cathedral around which the town grew up was built from locally quarried stone. Its pinkish-gold colour gives the Cathedral an air of warmth and intimacy. Visitors often express surprise, not only at seeing such a beautiful church so far North, but at the use of the term Cathedral, there being no bishops in the Presbyterian Church of Scotland. ('Cathedra' was the word for the bishop's seat.) When I explained to visitors that in Scotland we retained the title Cathedral for those buildings which prior to the Reformation were the seats of bishops, most accepted the explanation, but not all. One Sunday evening when an Englishman became almost aggressive, I reminded him, as graciously as possible, that Westminster Abbey is still called an abbey even though no longer ruled over by an abbot!

❄

Just before becoming minister of the Cathedral, the pride of the Cathedral's golden weathercock was considerably dented. Having been blown down in a January gale, the cockerel was taken away, repaired and repainted. The morning after it was returned to its perch at the top of the spire, the local people noticed that the cockerel had become a hen, wearing bra and pants. In the darkness one of the locals had scaled the spire to give the Cock o' the North a feminine look.

❄

In the 1830s the Duchess of Sutherland commissioned a 99-foot statue to be made of her late husband, the 1st Duke of Sutherland, and placed on the top of Ben Bhraggie, the hill overlooking Golspie and nearby Dunrobin Castle She also commissioned a life-size marble statue to be made and placed at the focal point of the chancel of Dornoch Cathedral. This so upset the local people that the vast majority of members left, for the same Duke had been responsible for the Sutherland Clearances, when thousands of their crofting friends had been evicted from their homes. What murmurs of disapproval there had been a few years before, when the Duchess had created a burial ground for the Sutherland family in the chancel of the Cathedral, and had installed in the central chancel window a marble slab telling the story of the Sutherland family. Many felt that the only course open to them was to leave the Cathedral. They went to church to worship a living Lord, not a dead Duke. Two lines of doggerel summed up the situation —

> *The auld kirk, the cauld kirk*
> *The kirk without the people.*

On the Cathedral doors they wrote,

> *The walls are thick, the folk are thin*
> *The Lord's come out and the de'il's gone in.*

❋

In the mid 18th century, trials of strength took place between the East coast men and those from the North. On one occasion when the event took place in Dornoch, a man from the North outdistanced the men from the East in throwing the heavy stone. Feeling was running so high that there was the real danger of rioting and disorder. (Substituting football for shot-putting, how modern it all sounds.) Word was quickly sent to the Cathedral minister, John Sutherland, who was a man of immense physical stature. He duly arrived on the scene. Without even taking off his cloak, he threw the stone further than the leading North Coast man, thus restoring peace to the local community.

❋

One of my most precious Dornoch memories concerns a young man who one Sunday slipped in at the back of the Cathedral just before the service started. He had lost his job. His wife had left him. He was at that lonesomest spot on earth, 'Wits End'. He had contemplated suicide. After the service he waited and spoke to me, wanting to start some kind of new life. 'This morning,' he said, 'you gave me back a feeling of real worth.' I am glad that day he did not run into a protagonist for atheism. If instead of being confronted with the Christian understanding of the meaning and purpose of life, and the Gospel of the second chance, he had been told there was no ultimate purpose in the universe, that he came from nothing, signified little and was going nowhere, would he have found in that the necessary stimulus to start again? I doubt it. There are many ways of expressing what is wrong with Britain today, but probably as profound as any is that many people, having lost their awareness of their importance in the sight of God, are now motivated by nothing greater than self-interest – and that is not healthy.

❋

At a Dornoch Burns Supper two of the speakers taking part were Ewan Currie of the Burghfield Hotel and Philip Rice the deputy rector of Golspie High School. In his introductory remarks the chairman Dick Ross commented on how the evening had the makings of being the strangest Burns Supper he had ever attended. Normally, he said the menu at a Burns Supper is Haggis and Neeps (turnips), but tonight it is Currie and Rice!

❋

During our time in Dornoch, my wife and I became friendly with Rosamunde Pilcher, the writer of such bestsellers as *The Shell Seekers* and *Coming Home*. Rosamunde had a holiday home overlooking the Cathedral. Aware of her great love of Dornoch, we were not surprised to learn that Dornoch became the setting for her last novel *Winter Solstice*, a story about a man called Oscar who lost his wife and daughter in a horrific car accident. Prior to their tragic deaths he had been organist in his local church in England, but thereafter he would have nothing more to do with the church. Shortly after Oscar moved to Dornoch (called Creggan in the novel), he was introduced to the local minister. (*That Rosamunde should choose the golf course for their meeting did nothing to help dispel the belief of my golfing friends in Glasgow that my call to Dornoch came not from the Cathedral but from the Royal Dornoch Golf Club!*) But so great had Oscar's hostility become towards the church, he gave the minister short shrift. Realising later how unnecessarily rude he had been, he called at the manse to apologise and explain the reason for his unacceptable behaviour. Having reached this point in her fascinating story, Rosamunde asked if I would read the manuscript and help her write the dialogue for this crucial meeting between the minister and Oscar. Obviously the loss of his wife and daughter would be the main topic of conversation. In my reply I shared with Rosamunde certain things I would try and introduce into such a conversation, and certain things that on no account would I say. In speaking with traumatised people like Oscar, I have always listened more than I talked, and tried to share with them my firm belief, that far from being the intentional will of God that people should die in such tragic circumstances, that God's must often be the first heart to break. What a wonderful job

94

Rosamunde did in taking some of the thoughts I had penned and weaving them into a moving dialogue. One of the many people who wrote to Rosamunde, a Marion McKinley, said,

> 'While reading Winter Solstice *I came upon the part where the minister is talking to Oscar about the tragic death of his daughter. Instead of telling Oscar that she is in a better place, and it was God's will, the minister said, "When your daughter died, God's was the first heart to break." This passage knocked me for a loop. I have been struggling with my faith since we lost our 39-year-old daughter to cancer. But believing in a loving God, I could not see how "He needed her more than we and her children did", which were the kind of things people were saying. I have read this passage many times and repeated it to our family and friends. You cannot believe how much peace it has given me. Thank you Rosamunde for making a difference in my life.'*

The oil-fired Aga in the Dornoch manse was my wife's pride and joy. No other cooker coped as well with the large Christmas turkey, or made as wonderful meringues. It also kept the large kitchen gloriously warm by pumping out heat even when blizzards affected the electrical power supply. What I did not know until recently was that the Swedish scientist who invented the Aga, Gustaf Dahlen, was awarded the Nobel Prize for physics. The award was not for inventing the Aga, but for designing an automatic gas light regulator for lighthouses. Dahlen was apparently not the judges' first choice. They wanted to award the prize jointly to Dr Edison and Dr Tesla for their research into transmitting electricity over great distances without major power losses. Edison was convinced Direct Current could be transmitted better than Alernating Current. Tesla favoured the latter. Though the technical case in favour of AC is unanswerable, Edison, rather than admit he was wrong, decided to denigrate his rival's system. The way he chose to do this was by making AC the basis of a new form of capital punishment. Edison secretly purchased AC equipment from Tesla's company for the manufacture of electric chairs. For a while he succeeded in getting Americans to associate AC with the horrors of electrocution. The tension between the two men became so great that when the Nobel Committee did some soundings to see if the two men would share the 1912 physics prize, Tesla refused. The committee decided instead to award it to Dahlen for his contribution to lighthouse safety.

We often took visitors to the Dornoch manse to the Whaligoe Steps located on the east coast, north of Dornoch. The 365 steps make it possible for people to descend the huge cliffs to a little harbour. In 1769 the local minister, Alexander Pope wrote, 'In this parish there is a haven for fishing boats called Whaligoe... The country people have made steps by which they go up and down, carrying heavy burdens on their back.' By the middle of the 19th century Whaligoe was a busy port, home to 35 boats. Many of the fishermen were local crofters who worked part time catching the valuable and very tasty 'silver darlings'. As you stop on the ascent, for a wee 'breather', you marvel at how the fishermen's wives carried the huge herring creels, some weighing over 100lb, up these steps, and then sometimes the further seven miles to Wick. What powerful women they must have been, for we are told they also carried their husbands out through the water to their boats, so that they could fish in relatively dry clothes. Without doubt the most amazing story about these strong women tells how they once rescued some half-drowned seamen from a boat which had been smashed trying to enter the narrow harbour. They not only carried them to their homes, they warmed them up by putting them into bed and then lying beside them! A unique cure for hypothermia! No wonder people speak of the uniqueness of Highland hospitality!

❋

Shortly after we moved from Glasgow to Dornoch in 1976, my son's new friend Gary called one morning to accompany him to school. On hearing Gary say excitedly, 'Neil, the swallows are back', I realised we were living in a quite different culture. The school's ornithological club, run by the headmaster, introduced Dornoch youngsters to the wonders of the bird life all around them. The headmaster, a Mr McCulloch, was well aware that life is very much what people are alive to, that the more spheres of healthy interest young people have, the fuller and more satisfying their lives will be.

❋

In 1976 the annual golf subscription for Dornoch youngsters was 25 pence per year! Like many local lads, my sons spent their school holidays, and later their university holidays, caddying. It was not only a healthy summer occupation, but a profitable one. One year, after he had been caddying for most of the summer, I inquired of Neil whether the golfers he had caddied for that day had been friendly and good players. 'Dad,' he said, 'it is certainly a bonus if they are friendly and play well, but it is more important that they should be reasonably quick!' On one occasion, after completing a five-and-a-half-hour round, an American golfer expressed the hope that his caddy, a man in his fifties, was not too tired. 'No, Sandy, 'but I am a bit homesick.'

✸

Many years later in his capacity as Director of the Scottish National Golf Academy, Neil was due to visit America. He wrote to inquire of the captain of the Brookline Country Club whether it might be possible for him and his brother Alistair, who at that time was living near Boston, to play their famous course, where the Ryder Cup was due to be played in the autumn. The captain phoned Neil, warmly inviting them to be his guests. When the captain learned during the phone conversation that Neil was a member at Royal Dornoch, he said, 'That is my favourite course. What is your connection with Dornoch?' When Neil told him that his father had been for many years the minister of the Cathedral there, the captain said, 'That is interesting. The last time I played Royal Dornoch, my caddie was a son of the minister.' When Neil and Alistair arrived at Brookline, the captain produced a photograph of himself with Alistair on the first tee at Dornoch. What a small world it is.

✸

Donald Ross, who was brought up in Dornoch, became to golf-course design what Telford was to bridges and Brunel to railways. On the Dornoch links, he and his brother Alec acquired considerable skill at the Royal and Ancient game. Regular attenders at church with their parents, they also acquired a balanced outlook on life. At the beginning of the 20th century Donald and Alec set off for America to further their golfing careers. There in 1907 Alec won the American Open. (Very few people in Dornoch are aware that one of their sons won this prestigious title.) Though Donald was also a fine player, he concentrated more on designing golf courses. More than 500 courses bear the Ross imprint. Golf was not however his first or only love. In the sandhills of North Carolina he not only built one of the truly great golf courses of the world, Pinehurst No 2, where the American Open is often played, he also became a founder member of the Pinehurst interdenominational village church. 'Golf is a fine game,' he once said. 'It has been my relaxation and livelihood since I was a little boy in Scotland. But when the game of golf becomes so all important and feverish and holier than anything else in life, then something has gone far wrong.' Donald Ross' words remind me of what another outstanding Scottish golfer Sandy Lyle said years later. In the years following his 'Open' and 'Masters' victories, Sandy began to lose his confidence and natural swing.

peting,' he said, 'wasn't anything like the fun it had once been.'
then he added, 'Playing badly is not however the end of the
ld. My seven-year-old son Quintin has had as many operations as
thdays, and when you see some of the poor kids in Great Ormond
reet hospital, reality and perspective set in very quickly.'

✳

Tom Watson said of his 24-hour visit to Dornoch, during which he
played three rounds of golf, 'It is the most fun I have had playing golf
in my life.' High praise indeed from a five-times Open champion. Even
if your drives are not flying straight and the putts not dropping, you
can still enjoy the panoramic views of the sandy beaches and the
Sutherland hills, and the wonderfully fresh sea breezes. There is
something magical about finishing a round of golf at Dornoch on a
June evening shortly before midnight.

On those Saturdays which were wedding free, I often made up a
foursome with Niall Currie, the owner of the Burghfield Hotel,
Dennis Bethune, a former professional, and the local professional,
Willie Skinner. The social aspect of these games — the chat and the
good natured banter was very appealing. Though none of us took
golf as seriously as we had once done, yet winning the pound at
stake was like winning the lottery. Willie's wife Mary kindly
managed the professional's shop during Willie's absence. On one
occasion when Willie went to put away clubs which a German
couple had rented in order to try golf for the first time on the nine-
hole course, he discovered that Mary had by mistake given them
right-handed irons and left-handed woods. We laughed at the
thought of them returning to Germany, saying, 'In Scotland they
play the woods one way, and the irons the other way.'

✳

Dornoch's debt to Andrew Carnegie, the American steel magnate —
or the Star-spangled Scotsman, as he was often referred to in
America — is considerable. To the Royal Burgh of Dornoch he
gifted the library in the High Street. His boast that the sun never
set on a Carnegie Free Library was justified, for his libraries, three
thousand in all, are to be found in all corners of the world —
Edinburgh, Pittsburgh, Dallas, Dunedin... The Dornoch library is
unique in that it is the only one to have Carnegie's library insignia,
'Let there be light', in Gaelic. To Dornoch Cathedral, he gifted a
pipe organ, and to the golf club a priceless silver shield for an open
competition — the only golf trophy I know to have two pictures of
the local church engraved on it!

✻

Andrew Carnegie spent five months each summer in Skibo Castle on the outskirts of Dornoch. It was there that most of his vast philanthropic work was carried out. The 364 million dollars he gave away would have to be multiplied by at least a hundred for one to appreciate their present-day value. We are told that Carnegie finally found it a great strain deciding which of the numerous appeals for financial help to accept and which to reject. On hearing how every week Carnegie received countless begging letters, Mark Twain, who was a close friend, decided to add one more. He wrote, *'Dear Sir and Friend, You seem to be prosperous these days. Could you lend an admirer a dollar to buy a hymn-book. God bless you if you do.'* Then Twain added a PS: *'Don't send the hymn-book, just the money.'* We don't, unfortunately, have a copy of Carnegie's reply. Normally when they corresponded they addressed each other as 'St Andrew' and 'St Mark'!

✻

Aware of the social havoc caused by excessive drinking, Carnegie offered his Skibo employees a 10% salary bonus at the end of the year if they signed the pledge. The majority did. But instead of making total abstainers of them, this offer resulted in a great deal of secret drinking. And as the local Dornoch shopkeepers knew well, many who had signed the pledge used the annual end of the year bonus, paid out when Carnegie was three thousand miles away in New York, to stock up for the New Year festivities.

✻

In the early 1900s, Rudyard Kipling, one of the most famous writers of his day, was a regular guest at Skibo Castle. Both he and Carnegie took up golf late in life. Though they were never more than happy hackers, both derived great enjoyment from the game. I sometimes wonder if it was from Kipling that Carnegie got the notion to take up golf. In 1892 when golf was still very much a novelty in the New World, Rudyard Kipling lived for a few years in an estate in Vermont. There he established a small golf course on the property, just as Carnegie later did at Skibo. Summer and winter alike, he would whack the ball around on this makeshift layout. The Nobel prize-winner's stay in Vermont was productive in several ways. Not only did he write there the classic *Just So Stories* and the *Jungle Books*, he also invented the red golf ball. This allowed him to play golf even through the North American snow and frost! There is no fool like an old fool!

During one of the fireside conversations in Skibo Castle with Andrew Carnegie's only daughter Margaret, she shared with me a fascinating story her father had told her about Rudyard Kipling. It concerned a circus elephant called Bozo. Shortly after Bozo was brought to Britain he tried three times to kill his new owner. Twice in the circus arena he had terrified the young people by bellowing furiously. Nothing his owner did seemed to calm Bozo. Finally the circus owner decided the elephant would have to be shot. To try and recoup some of the costs of bringing Bozo to this country he sold tickets for Bozo's execution. Crowds filled the circus tent on the Saturday morning. Bozo was behind bars in a large cage. Outside the cage was the ringmaster in top hat. With him were several men with army rifles. Bozo continued to bellow. Just before the ringmaster was about to give the signal to the firing squad, he felt a tap on his shoulder. Beside him stood a short man with a little moustache, thick glasses and a brown hat. 'Would you not rather keep the elephant alive?' he asked. 'Obviously I would,' said the ringmaster, 'but I cannot run the risk of getting hurt or someone else getting hurt. He is just a bad elephant.' 'You are wrong,' said the little man. 'Let me into the cage and I will show you that you are wrong. Look, I have brought a legal document freeing you from all responsibility should anything happen to me.' Having examined the document, the manager turned to the crowd. 'This man thinks he can calm and change Bozo. Let us see.' Taking off his coat, hat and glasses, the little man entered the cage. The silence in the arena was intense. When the steel gate opened Bozo gave an angry squeal. As the elephant moved towards the man, he stood his ground. The crowd could hear him speaking to the elephant, but they could not make out what he was saying. But gradually as the man spoke the elephant quietened down. Not only was the angry squeal gone, its huge body was no longer shaking. The big head began to wag from side to side. The little man then moved forward and began to pat Bozo's trunk. He then walked round the cage leading the animal by the trunk, all the time talking to him. The crowd began to cheer. When he left the cage the man said to the circus manager, 'There is nothing evil about Bozo. He is just homesick. I simply talked to him in Hindustani, the language he was accustomed to in India.' The little man collected his jacket, glasses and hat and disappeared. Looking at the legal document which he had in his hand, the ring master read the signature. The name on it was Rudyard Kipling. While working as a young reporter in India, Kipling had learned to speak Hindustani.

Growing Old Gracefully

We get better facial wrinkles from smiling and laughing than from frowning

It is more difficult to grow old gracefully than to grow up. 'To grow old,' said Albert Camus, 'is to pass from passion to compassion.' Would that it were always so. Most people grow neither better or worse as they get old — simply more like themselves. Their dominant characteristic tends to become more dominant.

✳

We must not identify old age and growing old. Growing old is an emotion which can come over a person at any age. Some people have it between the ages of 25 and 30! To be 70 years young is better than being 40 years old. Nobody grows old merely by living a number of years — people grow old by deserting their ideals. Years wrinkle the skin, but to lose our enthusiasms wrinkles the soul. Another way to keep the heart young is not to let one's thoughts live with the past, but to keep them in tune with life around us. We cannot help getting older, but we can help getting old. Hopefully we will die young as late as possible.

> *Though we go no more a dancing*
> *Late into the night*
> *The heart is still as loving*
> *And the moon is still as bright*

Louise Claspill expresses similar thoughts in her moving prayer:

> *Dear Lord,*
> *You changed my hands into crinkled tissue paper*
> *You draped my face with velvet folds and wrinkles*
> *My weighted body shouts, 'You're old!'*
> *But Lord,*
> *Inside, I think young. The child has survived.*

✳

Old people have at least one advantage over the young. Having been young, and having been old, we know both ages. Young people on the other hand only guess what it must be like to be old.

✳

The process of growing old is not all fun — heart and memory problems, waterworks and arthritic problems, the deaths of longstanding friends. Even though the minuses of the ageing process are numerous, the most common complaint about old age

101

is that it does not last long enough. For the elderly the only thing worse than having another birthday, is not having one. The geriatric logic behind some lines of doggerel appeals to me.

Take one good breath while still in bed
One cautious stretch from toe to head
If nothing hurts you must be dead

An elderly American Democrat declared that one of the problems of approaching ninety is that almost always there is some reason you want to live another year. At the start of 2004 he told a friend that he would like to live another year so that George W. Bush would no longer be President. Then he added, 'If he's re-elected I will have to live another four years!'

❋

You know you are getting older when your knees buckle, but your belt won't, when your back goes out more than you do, when you turn out the lights for economic rather than romantic reasons, when the little old lady you help across the road is your wife, when you sink your teeth in a Pavlova and they stay there. Time may be a great healer, but it is not a good beautician.

❋

The aging process has made my wife's arms shorter. When we got married she could put her arms right round me! About the time I celebrated my 70th birthday, people regularly said to me, 'You look wonderful.' What I think they meant was: 'For someone as old as you are, you don't look bad.'

❋

After parking her car, an elderly lady wound down the window so that her spaniel would have enough air. Pointing at the little dog lying in the back seat, she snapped, 'Stay. Stay.' Not seeing the dog, and thinking she was talking to the car, a passer-by said, 'Try using the handbrake.'

❋

There are three periods in retirement – 'Go-go', 'Go-slow', 'No-Go'.

❋

Pope John XXIII, the so-called caretaker Pope, who threw open the windows of the Vatican to let the fresh air in, wrote in his *Journal of a Soul*, 'The older I grow, the more clearly I perceive the dignity and winning beauty of simplicity in thought, conduct and speech; a desire to simplify all that is complicated and to treat everything with the greatest naturalness and clarity. I must strip my vines of all useless foliage and concentrate on what is true, just and loving.'

✳

I have known nights when I have sympathised with the old lady who said, 'I wish I was in bed without the trouble of going.'

✳

You are getting old when you get the same sensation from a rocking chair that you once got from a roller coaster.

✳

When George Burns was in his nineties and recovering from surgery, he let it be known that he intended to keep his stage appointment in Las Vegas. Asked why he was still performing at such a great age, he said, 'Well, I have got to earn some money to put away for my retirement.' Speaking on a television special, *George Burns' 95th Birthday Party*, George said, 'People are always asking me when I am going to retire. Why should I? I have got the best of both worlds – I am still making films and I am a senior citizen, so I can see myself for half-price.'

✳

A new broom sweeps clean, but the old brush knows the corners.

✳

An air steward tells how during a long night flight an elderly lady asked the head steward, 'How do our pilots know they are flying straight? It is so dark out there.' The steward pointed through one window to the light on the tip of the wing: 'Do you see that green light, madam?' When she nodded enthusiastically, he pointed through the opposite window to the other wing: 'Do you see that red light?' 'Yes,' she replied. 'Well,' said the steward, 'as long as we stay between these two lights, we are OK.'

✳

Shortly after his 92nd birthday, Chief Justice Oliver Wendell Holmes passed a very beautiful young woman as he walked with a friend in Washington DC. Turning to his companion, he said, 'Oh, to be eighty again!' That story reminded me of the old man who confided to his equally elderly friend, 'I'd love to live in the past. The trouble is I can't remember it.'

✳

A woman tells how she took her rather grouchy 90-year-old mother who was blind in one eye to an ophthalmologist. When during his examination the doctor held up three fingers and asked her, 'How many fingers do I have?' she snapped back, 'I hope you have five if you are going to operate on me.'

✻

A 92-year-old farmer from Crieff met me one day in Perth. 'Dr Simpson,' he said, 'do you believe in miracles?' When I asked why he asked that question, he said, 'You know how in the Second World War I lost the sight in one of my eyes. Well recently I was having some problems with my other eye. My GP referred me to the eye clinic. After examining my "good eye" the consultant inquired about what had happened to my other eye. When I told him the story, he asked if he could examine it.' Having done so, the consultant said, 'There is a possibility I could restore sight to your other eye. Would you let me operate on it as well.' With nothing to lose Mr Stewart readily agreed. When the bandages were removed, he was astonished to discover he could see with both eyes. 'Doctor,' he said, 'you have given me a problem. Because I lost the sight in my eye in the war, I have a war pension. What am I going to do?' When the doctor asked what his age was, and was told 92, he said, 'If I was you I would not do anything.'

✻

A Mr Vaughan tells how he and his wife were attending a business conference. One night at dinner, his wife who had great difficulty remembering names, twice asked him their table companions' names during the meal and again on their return to the hotel. In exasperation he chided her about her lack of attention. He ended his lecture by saying that he was surprised she could remember his name. With a mischievous twinkle in her eye she responded, 'Why do you think I call you "darling" most of the time?'

✻

When a woman used her banker's card for the first time in a cash machine, it rejected it. The message intimated she had used an incorrect pin number. 'But,' said her husband, 'I thought you used your date of birth as your pin number.' 'I did,' she said sheepishly, 'but I lied about my age and I can't remember which year I used.'

✻

John, who had heart and other medical problems, was given new pills by the doctor. He was told to take a red and yellow one each Monday. Then skip Tuesday. On Wednesday he was to take a red and an orange one. Then skip Thursday. On Friday a yellow and a red pill. Then skip Saturday and Sunday. Ten days later he was dead. When John's son asked his mother if he thought the new pills could have been the cause of death, his mother said, 'No, I think it was all the skipping he was told to do.'

✳

A retired gentleman told his friend that he had done a study of his wife's routine as she made breakfast. 'She made a lot of trips between the refrigerator, cooker, table and cupboards, often carrying only one item. I suggested she try carrying several things at once.' When his friend asked if it had resulted in saving her time, he replied, 'Actually, yes. It used to take her about twelve minutes to make breakfast. Now I do it in ten.'

✳

A husband whose mother-in-law was visiting promised to be home by five o'clock. Just before five he phoned and explained that he had had a hole in one, and that he and some of his golfing friends were having a celebratory drink. He would be about an hour late. When his wife went and explained to her mother what had happened, her comment was, 'I bet you he deliberately tried it.'

✳

Seeing the vast array of books lining the walls of my study, my grand-daughter Rhona asked if I had read them all. I told her I had read parts of most of them, and all of some of them. Some I said had not lived up to expectations, a few I had had difficulty understanding, but many others had taught me a great deal and given me hours of pleasure. One such book is an old book by the father of Alistair MacLean, the writer of such thrillers and bestsellers as *The Guns of Navarone*. For many years Alistair MacLean (Sr) was the minister of Daviot Church on the outskirts of Inverness. In his book *High Country*, he says many profound things, but perhaps none more profound than: 'When we are young we want to *do* things. When the middle years come, we want to *get* things. When the westward years appear, we want to *be* things' — to be fully human, to be alive to truth and beauty, free from self-seeking and self-glorification, a friend to many. Many in the westward years begin to realise that they are essentially human beings, not human doers or human getters, that a person is rich or poor according to what he or she is, not according to what they own. It is the heart that makes a person rich. When your adult children and grandchildren want to be with you, that is a priceless bonus.

✳

There is nothing more beautiful than cheerfulness in an old face.

✳

In Neil Munro's novel, *The Shoes of Fortune*, the priest Father Hamilton says to his young friend Paul Greig, 'Be good, be simple, be kind. 'Tis all I know. Fifty years to learn it and I might have learned it at my mother's lap.' Many, as they look back on their lives, so strangely mingled of wisdom and folly, stand aghast at the time it took them to realise that 'Being and Loving' are far more important than 'Getting and Spending'.

✳

Dr Mackintosh, the former professor of public health at the University of London, wrote the following letter to himself to be opened on his 65th birthday. Far from indulging in self-pity, he gives himself a well-placed and much-needed kick.

My Dear Mackintosh,

I hope you will profit from these few words of friendly advice. Certain undesirable tendencies in your character are already apparent, and I have little doubt they will become more marked as you grow older. In the first place you will become more talkative. Try to curb this fault, because it is an early sign of unwillingness to learn from younger people. It will lead you to a final inability to learn anything. Try to be a good listener. But you must really listen – not just turn your head and make gestures. Try to avoid prying into the affairs of young people, even on the plea that with all your experience you can help them. If they ask for your help in time of trial, give it in full measure, but not until asked. And do not try to attract sympathy to yourself.

There are also three qualities that you can develop as you grow older – courtesy, integrity and tolerance... By tolerance I do not mean an easy-going acceptance of everything that is done. I mean the capacity to understand the point of view of others, a willingness to argue without acrimony, and yet with spirit. By courtesy I mean the ability to put yourself in the place of other people. It is a rare and beautiful virtue. By integrity I mean wholeness of spirit.

The main practical thing to remember is that you are now 65 and on the point of retirement. For heaven's sake retire and do not persuade yourself that you are a special case. If you have kept body and soul active, a world of new interests lies before you. If not then you have no business to cling to office.

Now remember,

Yours faithfully,

James M. Mackintosh

✻

Aware of the many medical ailments which are part and parcel of the aging process — arthritic hips, cataracts, hearing difficulties — I told a group of ministers at a pre-retirement course, that I was tempted to change slightly the words of some of our best known hymns, to make them even more relevant for those nearing retirement. I would amend:

'Count your many blessings... ' to: 'Count your many *birthdays*, name them one by one'.

'Give me the Old Time religion', to: 'Give me the Old *Timer's* religion'.

Aware of the many dental problems associated with aging, I can think of no more appropriate hymn than: 'Crown him with many crowns'.

'Nobody knows the trouble I have seen,' I would amend to read: 'Nobody knows the trouble I have *seeing*'.

'O for a closer walk with God', to: 'O for a *slower* walk with God'.

'Courage brother do not stumble', to: '*Careful* brother do not stumble'.

To the hymn 'Go tell it on the Mountain', I would add '*(and speak up)*'.

To 'Guide me O Thou great Jehovah', I would add '*(for I've forgotten where I have parked the car)*'

'Blessed Assurance', I would amend to: 'Blessed *Insurance*'.

No amendment is needed to Narayan Tilak's hymn: '*One who is all unfit...* '

✻

A Prayer for the Aged: God grant me the senility to forget the people I never liked, the good fortune to run into those I do like; and the eyesight to tell the difference.

You'll Never Die Laughing

There are people who would rather be accused of shoplifting than of not having a sense of humour – especially those with little sense of humour! I often wish humour had been included in the five senses, for kindly humour greatly enriches all aspects of life. It helps us relax and see things more in perspective. It is good medicine.

The mobile phone has revolutionised our lives, turning millions into walking transmitters. You can hear the personalised ringtones of the omnipresent mobile in cinemas, bars, churches and even crematoriums. A railway carriage can sometimes be like a telephone exchange. Whereas parents used to ask their children, before setting out on holiday, 'Have you all been to the toilet?' many now ask, 'Has everyone got their mobile?' Mobile phones have invaded not just secondary schools, but primary schools as well. A Glasgow mother of a seven-year old was surprised to hear her son, whom she had just dropped off at school, phone home in a tearful voice: 'Mummy, I have had an accident.' Aware that he did not have a mobile phone of his own, she inquired where he was ringing from. His reply was not quite what she expected: 'From the breeks down.'

In front of a mother and her young son in the supermarket checkout was an amply built lady. When her pager suddenly sounded, the boy – who was obviously familiar with reversing alarms on vans – said, 'Look out, Mum. She is going into reverse.'

When the staff nurse answered the phone in Ward 4, the caller inquired after Walter Smith. When informed that he was improving each day, the caller asked, 'Do you think he might get home this week?' 'If there are no setbacks he could possibly get out on Friday,' said the nurse. The caller thanked her. Just before he rang off the nurse said, 'Can I say who is calling?' 'Yes,' he said, 'it is Walter Smith in Ward 4.'

A Directory Inquiries operator received a request from a man on a mobile phone. 'Can you give me the number for the Texaco Garage on the A3?' 'There are two such garages,' she said. 'Which one do you want?' 'The one,' said the inquirer, 'where I am locked in the toilet and cannot get out.'

A Patty Dunham tells how one night her boss and her family came over to her home to play cards. Shortly after they drove away at the end of the evening, Patty discovered that her boss had left her handbag in a corner. She was about to telephone her house, intending to leave a message, when her son reminded her that her boss had a mobile phone. As they dialled her mobile number, Patty marvelled at the technology that would alert them before they had gone far. A few seconds later a ringing sound came from the handbag lying near her!

The wisecrack about women of 35 who have remained so for years is attributed to Oscar Wilde, but in fact a document from 1739 records this exchange: 'Cousin, do you believe that I am in the right when I say I am but forty?' 'I ought not to dispute it, Madam,' replied he, 'for I have heard you say so these past ten years.'

Solicitors must be the butt of almost as many unflattering comments and jokes as clergymen. One I love concerns a young solicitor who was setting up in practice. He had a fine new office, but so far no clients. As he sat at his desk twiddling his thumbs there was a knock at the door. As he said, 'Enter,' he picked up the phone and began conversing with an imaginary client. Putting his hand over the mouthpiece, he asked the visitor to be seated. 'Sorry about that,' he said, putting the phone down. 'Very important High Court Case. How can I help?' 'I'm from British Telecom,' replied the visitor. 'I have come to connect your phone.'

Carl Field tells how his father, who was a solicitor, once took him to a fancy city restaurant. When the bill arrived there was a £2.50 charge for bread and butter. His father paid the bill, including the charge for the bread and butter. The next day, however, he sent a letter to the restaurant stating that this £2.50 charge was uncalled for. Enclosed in the same envelope was a £100 bill for legal services. Someone from the restaurant called immediately and asked what the £100 bill was for, that they had never requested legal services. His father replied, 'Two days ago in your restaurant, I never ordered any bread and butter.' The £2.50 was returned without delay.

A third lawyer story which exercised my chuckle muscles concerned a man who went to the local lawyer and asked how much he charged. When he was told it was £50 for three questions, the man said, 'Isn't that a bit steep?' 'I don't think so,' said the lawyer. 'Now, what is your third question?'

✳

It had been a good Saturday for the butcher. There was not much to be put back in the refrigerator. The chickens had sold especially well. The butcher had taken the only one left through to the back shop with the intention of taking it home. But just as he was about to close the shop, a well-to-do lady who lived at the other end of their country town came into the shop. He was surprised to see her, for he knew she normally bought her meat from the other butcher. She explained that her son had phoned to say that he and the family would be coming for Sunday lunch – did he have a chicken? Now instead of being honest and saying that her luck was in, that he had just one left, he said that would be no problem. Keen to make a good impression, he added, 'I always keep a fine selection of chickens.' When he brought out the only chicken he had, she said, 'You don't have a slightly bigger one?' 'Sure,' he said. Taking the chicken through to the back shop he blew into it and pulled its legs to make it look slightly bigger. Then taking it back through he said, 'I am sure that one will suit you.' She looked at it and then, to his horror, said, 'I tell you what, I will take both.'

✳

Dr Donald Mowatt, a past captain of Edzell Golf Club, tells how for many years they had problems with the low-lying eighth green. When the river, which runs beside the green, was in spate, the green and surrounding bunkers would often be flooded. Sam, the head greenkeeper, told Dr Mowatt one morning how the previous week he had found a 10lb 4oz salmon swimming in one of the greenside bunkers. When Dr Mowatt asked Sam what he had done with it, he was told he had thrown it back into the river. With a mischievous glint in his eye, Dr Mowatt said, 'Tell me, Sam, how did you know it was 10lb 4oz?'

✳

Another golf club had a member who was renowned for seldom buying a round of drinks. But one day in the clubhouse, to the amazement of his three golfing partners, he actually broke a £20 note to buy them a drink. Taken aback by this unexpected generous gesture, one of the members suggested that he had better be careful. He could be charged with breaking and entering! On hearing this, another member, a lawyer by profession, said it would be pointless charging him, as he would certainly get off lightly, it being so obviously a first offence.

※

A lady who had just learned to drive had trouble negotiating a small parking space. Luckily a passer-by stopped to help her. With the aid of his hand signals she managed to slip neatly into the space. She thanked the man. What she was too embarrassed to tell him was that she had actually been trying to get out of the space.

※

On an office notice board, the following slogan had been pinned, 'Veni, Vidi, Velcro – I came, I saw, I stuck with it.'

※

At a reception in Edinburgh Castle I enjoyed a chat with Bishop John Mone, the Roman Catholic bishop of Paisley. He told me how he was playing one evening at the Hamilton golf club. It was a slow round. Being on his own he had to wait at almost every shot. Two much younger men, who were holing out on the 9th green as he waited on the tenth tee, suggested they might join up. He introduced himself simply as John. He played the inward half that night better than he had ever done, holing out in 2 at both short holes. As they were playing the 17th, one of the young men asked him what he did for a living. When he told them he was a Roman Catholic bishop that was a real conversation stopper! The next question was about the weather!! Later he heard that one of the men had been asked in the clubhouse who they had been playing with. When he replied, 'A bishop,' the inquirer asked, 'Which bishop?' Recalling John's two birdies at the short holes, he said with a twinkle in his eye, 'I would not be surprised it if was Bishop Tutu.'

※

A Mr Davidson tells how when the window cleaner called for payment, he asked him if he had climbed through the upstairs window and used the toilet. 'Yes,' he said, 'I was absolutely desperate. I hope you don't mind.' 'Not at all,' said Mr Davidson, 'But next time please unlock the bathroom door before you climb back out.'

※

Margaret, who is a member of Cathcart Castle Golf Club, loves baking apple pies. Whenever there is a coffee morning in the club, the church or the community, Margaret will gift several home-baked pies. Knowing of her generosity, another member of the club, who was to be away from home for several weeks, told

Margaret to help herself to the apples in her garden. As she did so, she noticed in the garden a plum tree also laden with fruit. Aware that the plums would fall and rot before the owner returned, she decided to gather them as well and bake some plum pies. When the owner returned Margaret thanked her for the apples. Then she added, 'I hope you did not mind, but I took the plums as well.' To Margaret's horror her friend said, 'But we don't have a plum tree.' She had been in the wrong garden!

*

One night at a party, a freelance photographer who takes great pride in his work was introduced to an extremely pompous gentleman who wrote a weekly piece for a publication that had just used one of his pictures. After telling the photographer that he had liked the 'rather interesting' composition and tones he had used in his latest work, the columnist said, 'You must have a good camera.' The photographer, after congratulating the man on his article, added, 'You must have a good word processor.'

*

Those who met Mr Duguid did not quickly forget him. Blind himself, he worked tirelessly in the West of Scotland to raise funds for Guide Dogs. What a hearty laugh and wonderful sense of humour he had. He once told how many people have the mistaken idea that it is the dog that guides the blind person. But of course all the dog will do is avoid objects, and stop when it comes to a road-crossing. It does not know whether to turn right or left. Mr Duguid knew almost every road in Glasgow, but he was not as familiar with the Edinburgh streets. One day as he was going with his guide dog to speak at an Edinburgh church, he got lost. Hearing boys' voices nearby, he asked them how to get to the church. Not long after one wee lad started to give him directions, his friend interrupted him: 'It is not him you talk to, it is the dog.'

*

At the Joint Services Defence College, a discussion took place concerning the chiefs of the three services. Army and RAF members expressed concern that the titles of their respective chiefs were not as illustrious as that of the Royal Navy's *First Sea Lord.* Sympathetic naval colleagues suggested with tongue in cheek that the Army's top man might be known as 'First Landlord' and the RAF's top man as 'Lord of the Flies'.

*

Writing of his experiences in Auschwitz, the psychiatrist Victor Frankl told how suicidal despair was the greatest enemy in the camp. Living starved and half naked in that dsperate situation of human folly and sin, he found humour, which admittedly sometimes lasted only a few seconds, to be truly a godsend. He tells how one freezing cold night a band of Jewish prisoners were marched up and down. Their guard ordered them to repeat after him the name of each location. Marching down one path, the guard called out 'Goering Strasse'. At the next path when he shouted, 'Goebbels Allee', the prisoners replied 'Goebbels Allee' They reached the open field where they stood for roll call. The guard shouted out 'Hitler Platz', *platz* meaning square in German, but what the guard did not know was that in Yiddish, *platz* means 'drop dead!' Not surprisingly the Jewish prisoners shouted with great fervour, 'Hitler Platz.'

✳

The Queen, who had a great admiration for Harold Macmillan, offered him a hereditary earldom on his retiral as Prime Minister. This would have entitled him to membership of the House of Lords. But he refused. Recalling his crofter ancestry, he said it would not be 'in the family style'. But when on his 90th birthday Her Majesty once again made the offer, he accepted. Asked to explain his change of heart, he said, 'I have gone blind; and in the House of Lords it really does not matter if you are blind!' Then with tongue in cheek he added, 'or deaf or dumb.'

✳

A lady who had moved into an attractive cottage which showed her antique furniture to advantage, agreed to show a local women's group round her home. A friend who had offered to help her provide tea told her later how she had overheard one woman say to another, 'I should bring my daughter to see this house. She is always grumbling about her furniture. It would do her good to see how some people make do with this old stuff.'

✳

A customer in a restaurant heard a woman saying, 'No, you will not have an ice-cream, and that's final.' Turning, she was surprised to see a stylish young woman all by herself.

✳

Golf has more than its fair share of humorous stories. The Scottish comedian Andy Cameron tells of being invited to play in a celebrity pro-am golf tournament at Haggs Castle in Glasgow. He was nervous about taking part for he had not long taken up golf. As he was

113

practising on the putting green an official came over and told him Jimmy Tarbuck had phoned to say that he was caught up in traffic and would not make his allotted tee-time. The official wondered if Andy would take his place. Going over to the first tee he discovered he was playing with Sandy Lyle. The starter proudly announced, 'On the tee Sandy Lyle, the present American Masters champion, and former Open Champion.' Sandy's drive went soaring into the sky, on and on and on. Then the starter announced. 'On the tee Andy Cameron, Scotland's well known comedian.' Andy moved forward, hands and knees shaking, desperately hoping he would at least get his drive off the tee. Just before he started his back swing, a Glasgow voice was heard to shout, 'Come on wee man, put it past him.'

✳

Some years ago, at the close of a Sale of Work in my Glasgow Church, two members of the youth group came and said they would like to make me a present. They explained that on the bookstall, there had been a book which they felt was just right for me. It was not a book about the Christian faith, but a book by the American golfer Tommy Bolt who won the US Open in 1958, a book entitled *How to Keep your Temper on the Golf Course.* That Tommy Bolt, with his short fuse and Vesuvian temper, should have written such a book seemed to me rather like Saddam Hussein writing about how to get along with the Americans. Bolt's putter was reputed to have spent more time in the air than Lindbergh ever did. In his book, perhaps with tongue in cheek, Tommy Bolt claims he did not really have a worse temper than other golfers, that his fiery reputation stemmed from the fact that his surname had such close links with words like 'thunder' and 'lightning'. Whenever as a young professional he had lost his temper, the press were ready with their headlines 'LIGHTNING BOLT STRIKES AGAIN'. What Tommy Bolt did have was a 'wind problem' − a different kind of 'wind problem' from that normally associated with links golf. Quite often before driving off in a tournament, he would break wind noisily and pungently on the first tee. At one tournament, after several warnings, he was finally fined and penalised two strokes by the PGA. When he was informed of the penalty, instead of losing his temper, he said, with a twinkle in his eye, 'Should I not just have been penalised one stroke? That was an air shot!'

✳

A friend, who had attended a golf week, had received instruction in iron play, chipping and putting. On the fourth night he was overheard to say to his dinner companion, 'I am skipping the lesson on driving tomorrow. It is the only part of my game I have got left.'

Think on These Things

In his book *A Guide for the Perplexed* the philosopher E. F. Schumacher tells how, on a visit to Leningrad before the breakup of the Soviet Union, he consulted a map to find out where he was. From where he stood he could see several enormous churches, yet there was no trace of any of them on the map. Noticing the puzzled look on his face, the guide and interpreter explained, 'We don't show churches on our maps.' On hearing this Schumacher was even more puzzled. He pointed out that one church was clearly marked. 'Oh, but that is a museum, not what we call a living church. It is only the living churches we do not show.' Schumacher then offers a personal comment on this anomaly: 'It occurred to me that this was not the first time I had been given a map which failed to show many things I could see right in front of me. All through school and university I had been given maps of life and knowledge on which there was hardly a trace of many of the things that I most cared about and that seemed to me to be of the greatest possible importance to the conduct of my life.'

✳

Stephen Fry recalls how he walked off a London stage one night in the middle of a long run of a play, and disappeared for several days. 'I just suddenly felt I don't know what I am doing here. I felt as if I had been on a highway in the fast lane and suddenly realised that though I was in a very fine car and travelling incredibly fast, I had absolutely no idea where I was going.' He not only survived the crisis, he learned from it. 'I knew what I wanted to do. I just did not know what I wanted to be.'

✳

A headmaster for whom I had a high regard told of an insurance agent who called at his home. The agent quickly made several complimentary comments about their furniture. 'That old table must be worth a pretty penny... And that china cabinet and silver candlesticks. They are worth something. I hope they are fully insured.' When the headmaster told him they were insured, the agent asked for how much. When he quoted a certain amount, the agent laughed: 'Good gracious, that is not nearly enough.' When Mrs Joyce learned that the valuation he put on their possessions would add several hundred pounds more to the annual premium, she said, 'We don't have that kind of spare money.' On hearing this, the agent leant forward and said, 'Don't you realise that we are talking about the fundamentals of your life?' For Mrs Joyce that was the final straw. 'That is where you are wrong,' she said. 'Fundamentals indeed. There are far more important things than furniture, candlesticks and china cabinets.'

✳

When actress Sophia Loren sobbed to Italian film director Vittorio De Sica about the theft of some of her jewellery, he said, 'Listen, Sophia. There is one great truth I have learned about life. It is this — never cry over anything that can't cry over you.'

✳

A university student caught up with an older man who was out jogging on an American beach. Across the student's T-shirt were the words, 'Help stamp out virginity'. After running together for some time, the older man felt he had to say something: 'That is an unusual T-shirt,' he said. The student beamed and said, 'Thanks.' 'Can I make a suggestion?' said the man. 'When you go home take it off very carefully, and put it in a drawer. And some years from now when you are married and when that first young man comes to your home to take your daughter out on her first date, give him a present of that T-shirt.' The student looked angrily at the man, turned around and ran off down the beach. The following day the older man saw the student again. This time he was wearing a university T-shirt. Give the young man credit, he came over and said, 'Mister, I don't know who you are, but I want you to know that I binned that T-shirt. I guess I had not really thought it through.' Summing up his experience of life, Somerset Maughan said, 'I have gone a long way round to discover what everyone else knew already.' I suspect that in the not too distant future, society will have to reconstruct the moral code that many have so assiduously eroded, or gleefully binned.

✳

When the London *Times* asked a number of writers to write a short essay about 'What's Wrong with the World?' G. K. Chesterton's signed reply was not only the shortest, but the most to the point: '*Dear Sir, I am.*' On another occasion he told of a professor of philosophy who spent a great deal of time proving that life really was not worth living, until one day somebody accidentally fired a gun and the bullet passed through his hat. When that happened he ran for his life, thereby demonstrating that a person's behaviour is more powerfully influenced by his emotions than his intellect. We are nothing like as rational or logical as we often imagine ourselves to be. How most of us vote is determined more by our feelings than our intellect. Most arguments in pubs, clubs or homes about

116

politics and religion are about feelings, suspicions, preferences and long-standing prejudices.

❋

Smiles cannot be bought, begged, borrowed or stolen, for they are no earthly good to anybody until they are given away. To break our face into a warm smile is one of the loveliest things we can do for another person. Has it ever struck you that most advertisements for wristwatches show them with their hands pointing to ten minutes past ten, never twenty minutes past eight. When the hands are at 10.10, the watch-face gives the appearance of smiling, whereas when they are at 8.20 they remind you of a face with an unhappy sulk! The memory of a smile can last a long time. It can foster a great deal of goodwill. Nobody needs a smile so much as those who feel they have none left to give. A genuine smile at the right time is about the best thing I know for oiling the machinery of life. What messages and warm emotions are communicated. What delight a baby's first smile brings to its parents. Doting grandparents stand enraptured. I often wonder how many romances have been started by a stray smile in the passing. The best smiles are unplanned. When a smile is natural, the eyes and corners of the mouth join in the fun. How much more attractive they are than the unbidden smiles summoned by the photographer: 'Smile please.' When a smile does not come naturally we never look our best. We often in fact look foolish, instead of friendly. You can usually tell when people are smiling for effect, or using smiles as a sales tool. Their prime concern is to convince you they are nice guys, when sometimes they are anything but. The eyes are vacant and unengaged, the cheeks are slack, the lips scarcely lift.

❋

Whereas adolescents today jiggle and shake separately when they dance, dancing in my teenage years was a socially regulated kind of syncopated grappling. Though I was no Fred Astaire, I was keen to have as my dancing partners girls with looks approximating to those of Audrey Hepburn. In my teenage years girls sat demurely along the wall of the dance hall, waiting for a male to inquire, 'May I have this dance?' or less gracefully, 'Are you for up?' I can vividly recall rushing across the floor to get the partner of my choice for the last waltz. How thrilled I was if she accepted and agreed to let me walk her home. In the weeks before the school Christmas dance the gym teacher would try and teach us Scottish country dances such as the St Bernard's Waltz, the Dashing White Sergeant, the Eightsome Reel and the Gay Gordons (not the *Happy Gordons* as the politically correct insist today). We were taught not to tread on each other's toes, when to lead and when to follow, and how to cooperate with others in group dances like the eightsome reel. Not bad lessons for life.

✳

A gunman entered a Florida open prison and robbed an inmate of a stereo, television set and forty dollars in cash. 'The whole inmate population is still in shock,' said the governor. 'If you are not safe from armed robbery in prison, where are you safe?'

✳

C. A. Joyce, the headmaster of an Approved School in England, recalled a lad who caused him and other staff members endless problems. When Richard one day told Mr Joyce that he thought the Ten Commandments were just a load of rubbish, sensing that it was pointless arguing with him, Mr Joyce said, 'OK, Richard, you and I will dispense with them.' That night Mr Joyce went into his room and removed Richard's stamp album and football boots from his locker. In a letter addressed to Richard, which arrived the following morning, Mr Joyce found some money. He took it out before re-sealing the letter. (*It was customary then for headmasters of Approved Schools to read all the mail that arrived at the school.*) Richard finally stormed into his office and said, 'Sir, somebody is stealing.' 'So what?' said Mr Joyce. Opening his drawer he took out Richard's stamp album, football boots and the money. 'Richard, as there are no rules against stealing, I took them.' 'No rules against it?' he protested, 'Well there jolly well ought to be,' 'Richard, there used to be a rule "*You shall not steal*", but you remember we agreed to give it up.' 'Well,' he said, 'I think we had better have that one back.'

Mr Joyce tells how a few days later he told Richard that the evening meal was going to be delayed an hour, when in fact it was not. He also told him he was free to do something, but when Richard did it, he got into trouble from another member of staff for doing it. Finally Richard said, 'Sir, you told me lies.' 'I know I did,' said Mr Joyce, 'but the need to tell the truth was another of those silly commandments we agreed to get rid off – not bearing false witness.' 'Well,' said Richard, 'I think we had better have that one back as well.' Mr Joyce went on to tell how he got four of the Commandments back at Richard's request.

✳

A businessman tells of visiting a supermarket on his way home. In the car park he met a friend. While they were chatting, a woman

118

approached, pushing a trolley stacked high with melons. What he feared happened. The trolley overturned and hit his car, denting his door. Before commenting on the damage he helped the woman pick up the melons that had scattered. After they were all back in the trolley she turned and said, 'Thank you, but I must go now before the owner of the car arrives.'

✳

Few stories are more profound than Leo Tolstoy's short story, *How Much Land Does a Man Need?* The story concerns a Russian peasant by the name of Pahom, who dreamed of owning land of his own. He worked until he was able to purchase a few acres. This kindled his appetite for owning more land. He kept adding a few acres here, a few acres there. Eventually he came upon a vast territory owned by the Bashkirs, a people who lived on the steppes by a river, in felt-covered tents. The tribe offered him as a gift, all the land he could encompass in a day. The man set out at dawn. He walked in ever-widening circles at a breathless rate. As the sun began to set, panic set in. He was too far from the starting point to complete the circuit. All would be lost. Pahom finally died from exhaustion. The story ends with these words: 'Pahom's servant picked up the spade and dug a grave long enough for Pahom to lie in, and buried him in it. Six feet from his head to his heels was all the land he needed.'

✳

The Rev Jeremiah Horrocks, the brillant young amateur astronomer, was the first person to predict accurately the passage of the planet Venus across the sun. The year was 1639. He was just twenty-two at the time. Telescopes were invented just before he was born. The dilemma for Jeremiah was that his predicted date was Sunday 24th November. Being an Anglican minister he was torn between his early morning and early evening church duties and his desire to observe this unique astronomical occurrence. Jeremiah felt obliged to put church duties before his hobby. He would observe the sun in the interval between the services. He was rewarded by seeing the black dot on the sun's disc shortly before sunset, when the sun was low in the sky. This dedicated young astronomer died a few years later while still in his twenties. A tablet to his memory in Westminister Abbey bears a Latin sentence from his astronomical work *Venus in Sola Visa*. Translated, the epitaph reads, 'Called away to higher things which it was not proper to neglect because of lesser things'.

✳

The Las Vegas strip is two and a half miles of neon signs, bars, restaurants, hotels, nightclubs and casinos. At the heart of it is the Coca-Cola building, built to resemble an old-fashioned Coke bottle. In the theatre there you can learn about the advertising history of the company. For many people their favourite Coca-Cola advert is of the little boy who comes up to his football idol – the most famous American footballer of his day, Joe Green. Mean Joe Green, as he was known had just finished a hard game. As he is about to enter the dressing room the little boy offers him his Coke. Mean Joe, who normally had little time for kids or autograph hunters, accepts. The audience feels the relief that comes to Joe Green's dry throat as he drinks the whole bottle without stopping. When he finishes he does not say anything – not even, 'Thanks'. As the rejected kid walks away, Mean Joe strips off his jersey and tosses it to the boy. A big smile comes over the wee lad's face – 'Gee thanks,' he says. The boy's generosity softened the heart of even someone as mean as Joe Green. (When the advert was being filmed Joe had to drink more than twenty bottles of Coca-Cola before managing a whole one without burping!)

✳

Lord Kelvin was one of Scotland's most outstanding scientists. His house in the quadrangle of Glasgow University was one of the first houses in the world to have electricity. Lord Kelvin supervised the installation. One day while working with the labourers in the trench outside the house, one of his second-year students passed. Not recognising Lord Kelvin in his old coat and cap, he said rather superciliously, 'What do you know about electricity, old boy?' Lord Kelvin, who was at that time one of the world's leading authorities on electricity, looked up and said, 'Not very much, my son.'

✳

O'Henry, in his story *The Pendulum*, tells of a couple who lived in a drab flat. Katy the wife was alone all day. Every night about eight, after the evening meal, her husband would reach for his hat, and she would ask, 'Now where are you going, I'd like to know, John Perkins?' Always she got the reply, 'Thought I'd drop up to McCloskey's and play a game or two with the fellows.' One night John came home to find Katy absent. She had left a cold supper and a note saying that she had received word her mother was ill, and she would contact him tomorrow. Suddenly John felt her absence terribly. How could he have left her alone so often? He resolved that when she came back it would be different. He would stay at home in the evenings. Just then Katy returned. She had been called away on a false alarm. John was delighted. About an hour later he glanced at the clock. It was just after eight. Reaching for his hat, he walked to the door. 'Now where are you going, I'd like to know, John Perkins?' asked Katy. 'Thought I'd drop up to McCloskey's,' said John, 'and play a game or two with the fellows.'

❊

When Lloyd George remarked that the most dangerous feat is to attempt to cross a chasm in two jumps, a friend replied that if you could only jump fifteen feet and the chasm was fifty feet across, one jump was not a safe endeavour either. In that case it would be better not to jump at all, but walk down and then climb up the other side one step at a time. Have we valuable insight into management here? Some changes have to be achieved in one jump, or they will not go through at all. But at other times, easy does it.

❊

A fruit grower in California told how he insured the quality of his pear crop. In addition to getting the best trees, and treating the soil according to the best knowledge available, he sprayed not only his own orchard, but also the orchards on all four sides of his property in order to make sure that his trees would have clean air. His golden rule for producing good fruit was: 'You shall spray your neighbour as yourself.'

❊

During the Cold War when many anxious Americans were building nuclear shelters, a lady in Palo Alto in California sent a cheque for several thousand dollars to the United Nations. She said in her letter to the Secretary General that her donation was what it would cost to build a private fallout shelter. She said she believed it was better to use her money to strengthen an organisation struggling to prevent war. Would that her tribe had increased.

❊

During a visit to Edinburgh, Sir Winston Churchill was introduced at a social gathering to one of Edinburgh's finest ministers, Dr George Gunn. When Mr Churchill learned that each Sunday Dr Gunn preached to about 600 people, he said, 'If I were to speak twice a Sunday in the same place on my subject, politics, at the end of six months there would be no one there to listen to me.' I believe the explanation lies not in oratorical ability, but in the immortal longings there are in people. Some time ago I came across a song written in the 1980s when Russia was still officially not just communist, but to a marked degree atheistic. It was a song written and sung by a young Soviet metal band called 'Black Coffee'. 'See the wooden churches of Russia, feel their warped and ancient walls; come close and ask them about life. In these timbers beats a heart, lives a faith. Hush, hear the heartbeat.' Even under the frozen icecap of Soviet denial, the immortal longings stirred. Full barns may satisfy cattle, but not people. We have deeper hungers, hungers which food and drink and political doctrines cannot ultimately satisfy.

✳

A John Macfarland recalls how he spent several months one summer working in the slums of Chicago. Later he told the members of a small community church what he had seen, the degrading poverty, the injustice and prejudice, and how it had shocked him. After the service a wealthy member of that church, who had spent most of his working life in Chicago, said, 'Don't worry about it, John. You will get to the place where that sort of thing won't bother you any more.' How much human misery and pain could be avoided, how much finer this world would become, if we retained in middle age and old age our youthful ideals and concern. As Albert Schweitzer said, 'It is through the idealism of youth that we catch a sight of truth, and in that idealism we possess a wealth we must never exchange for anything else.'

✳

When the outstanding Scottish dance band leader Jimmy Shand found himself top of the video charts, he was telephoned by a radio reporter: 'Mr Shand, you must be ecstatic to be top of the charts at this stage in your life.' After a long pause, the accordion maestro from Auchtermuchty, with a deadpan face, uttered these memorable words: 'I've never been ecstatic in my life.' How impoverished our lives would be without moments of ecstasy, moments when we are surprised by life and delight in life. I have long believed that we ought to measure life, not by the number of breaths taken, but by the number of times we hold our breath in wonder – and ecstasy! I don't want to walk solemnly and arthritically towards the cemetery. I want to hop, skip and jump. So did Emily Dickinson. '*Take all away from me, but leave me ecstasy.*'

✳

Though only a minority of young people act out the violence they view on the silver screen, many more are, I believe, desensitised by scenes of gratuitous violence and degrading sex. The film *Scarface* exposed viewers to more than two hours of torture, gore and obscenity. The video-game *Manhunt* depicted a convicted murderer

122

being ordered by a demented film director to kill people in as gruesome a fashion as possible. The progression seems to be ever downward. I wonder how a desensitised next generation will rate even more violent video-games and films, and what effect they will have on troubled young people from unstable homes. Abraham Lincoln was surely right when he said, 'The real power in a nation lies not with those who shape its laws, but with those who shape its public opinion.' From an early age the values and images of the media enter the minds and bloodstream of the young. Unfortunately it is all too often the worst values that are on display, the best rarely whispered. A mother, concerned about what her teenage daughter had been watching on television, thought she had better sit down and have a chat with her. 'I hope you realise that most people at the end of their first date, don't just jump into bed with each other.' 'I know,' she replied. 'They always have a drink first.' Two decades ago those in the organic movement, who warned of the dangers of feeding cattle to cattle and the use of vast amounts of herbicides and pesticides, were caricatured. But the tide began to turn when cattle started dying of mad cow disease, when rivers became polluted by the use of vast amounts of pesticides and herbicides. I hope it will not be long before the media also stop caricaturing those who protest that we ought to treat young people's minds as gently as their stomachs.

✳

The controversial wall being built to separate Israel from Palestine reminds me of the child's question, 'Does God draw the lines around the countries?' The answer is an emphatic No. More often than not they have been the result not of providence, but of a variety of imperial, military and colonial takeovers. That was true of most of the African nations. It was true of the two Koreas. Was it God's idea to create two Irelands? Though we cannot totally undo the past, the future is ours to shape.

✳

In a modern Western, a cowboy says, "'Twasn't preaching and praying that made me a better man, but one or two people who believed in me more than I deserved. I hated to disappoint them.' I remember hearing of a man who had got a complex new hot-water system for his house. Right from the day of installation there were problems. He tried for weeks to get the firm to return and fix it. When a mechanic did finally come, he was the most sullen person imaginable. His body gave off a smell that matched his attitude. The homeowner was tempted to tell him exactly what he thought of him and his firm. But then he thought to himself: this fellow was in a bad mood before he got here; perhaps he is not feeling well, or has major problems at home. So instead of getting angry with the mechanic, he said, 'I bet it is really exhausting running all over town, working on fouled-up equipment in this hot weather.' On hearing this, the mechanic's attitude changed. Here was someone who at least tried to understand him. He not only made the necessary repair, but returned the following day to check it was still working properly.

❋

On a British Airways flight from Johannesburg in the mid-1980s, a middle-aged, prosperous, white, South African woman found herself seated next to a black man. She called the flight attendant to complain. 'I cannot possibly sit next to this kaffir. I want another seat.' Asking the woman to calm down, the attendant said she would see if there were any other seats available, but warned that the flight was very full. When she returned a few moments later she informed the lady that the only seat available was in the business class section. On hearing this, a smug, self-satisfied grin quickly appeared on her face, but it disappeared just as quickly when the attendant turned to the black man and said, 'The captain would like you to have it.'

❋

Start the day running and you never catch up. More nerves are frayed, more duodena ulcerated, by breakfast on the run and a hectic dash to the office than by any other factor. Nature reinforces this lesson. Dawn comes slowly. It is unhurried, almost catlike, slowly stretching and opening its eyes before it gets to its feet.

❋

People who show me their wealth are like beggars who show me their poverty; they are both looking for alms from me — the rich man for the alms of my envy, the poor man for the alms of my guilt.

❋

Civility is important in the life of any organisation. A good motto for any organisation might well be: 'We agree to differ; we resolve to love; we unite to serve.'

❋

Nicholas Evans in his book *The Smoke Jumper* tells of two hungry boys in a restaurant. The waitress brings each an empty plate and a short time later two steaks, one considerably bigger than the other. Jo thinks, 'Ah-ha, I know what to do.' He picks up the plate with the steaks and offers it to Mo. He assumes that Mo will be too polite to take the big steak. But that is exactly what Mo did. He took the big one, and proceeded to eat it. Jo was so mad that there was smoke coming out of his ears. Seeing the anger on Jo's face, Mo asked him what was wrong. 'If you must know,' said Jo, 'I am mad with you. I offered you the two steaks and you took the big one.' Mo says, 'Well, what would you have done if I had given you the choice?' And Joe says, 'Well, being polite, I would have taken the smaller one. And Mo says, 'Well, what is your problem? That is what you got.'

※

People who are generous on a one-to-one basis often fail to exhibit a similar generosity of spirit on community issues. The term NIMBY, 'not in my back yard' — which has made its way into the dictionary — stands for someone who is willing to let things happen, like the building of a new road, or a new home for recovering drug addicts, so long as it does not adversely affect their locality. Likewise we want the convenience of air travel, but not the noise of planes overhead. We want more prisons, but not near the suburb where we live. We want our rubbish removed and burned, but are opposed to the incinerator being located in our neighbourhood. We want 'greener' electricity, but not wind-farms in nearby hills.

※

As a young minister I often got frustrated by interruptions. I would be working on some article or sermon or speech which I thought was extremely important. Then suddenly the doorbell or phone would ring. Sometimes it was a young couple wanting to arrange a wedding, or a young lad wanting a character reference or a passport form signed, or a daughter whose father had died, or a mother of rebellious teenagers, wondering if she could cope much longer. Whatever the nature of the interruption, by the time I returned to my desk, my train of thought was broken. When I was just beginning to pick it up again, the phone would ring once more. It took me several years to realise that these interruptions were in fact my work — making time to listen to those at their wits' end, to share the happiness of the parents of a new baby, to welcome the visitor and the stranger. That I came to see that is what the ministry, and life is all about, and that if we ever become too busy for people, we are too busy. Dr Niebuhr once told us, how as a young professor he overworked until he had a serious breakdown. He later said he ought to have seen the warning signs, the clearest of which was when his students started apologising for bothering him. When we become exasperated by interruptions, we should

125

remember that their frequency may be an indicator of the contribution we are making to our common life. Only those who have the capacity to help are interrupted. One of the most awful things that could happen would be to become so independent, so unhelpful, so unneighbourly that nobody would ever interrupt us, that we would be left comfortably alone.

❄

I suspect that laziness, not necessity, has sometimes been the mother of invention, that we owe a tremendous debt to some of those who had a talent for doing as little as possible! Being inherently lazy, did they wrack their brains to think of easier ways of doing things? Was it someone who was too lazy to push who invented the wheel? Observing a circular stone running down a hill, did someone get an idea for avoiding hard work? I also wonder if it was someone who wanted to avoid having to row a boat, who invented the sail.

❄

When Seth Mouton was invited to give the graduating address at Harvard University, he listed a great number of outstanding Harvard graduates – John Adams, Theodore Roosevelt, Helen Keller, John F. Kennedy. 'These distinguished people,' he said, 'have one thing in common. They are all dead.' He then went on to issue a call for the new graduates to live for as noble goals in their day. He reminded them that success is not making a lot of money, but blazing new trails, making the most of one's best, doing what we can to enrich the lives of others and the world. I would say Amen to that.

❄

In 1947 when André Gide, one of France's most brillant writers, received the Nobel prize for literature, he was asked who was France's greatest writer ever, he replied, 'Victor Hugo.' Then he added, 'Alas!' I love Hugo's description of the bishop in *Les Misérables*. 'When he had money he visited the poor. When he had none he invited the rich.' A delightful Robin Hood!

❄

Anna Quindlen, the American columnist and novelist, concluded her graduation address to the students of Villanova University by telling them how one of her best teachers had been a man she met one December day on the boardwalk at Coney Island. She was doing a piece about how the homeless survive in the winter. The man's schedule involved making his home near the boardwalk when the summer crowds were gone, and sleeping in a church when the temperature went below freezing. When she asked him why he did not go to one of the shelters, he replied, staring at the ocean, 'Look at the view, young lady. Look at the view.' Anna then told the students, 'Every day in some little way I try to do what he said. I try to look at the view. That is the last thing I have to tell you today, words of wisdom from a man with not a dime in his pocket. "Look at the view."'

❋

Three kinds of people try me sorely — those who are always serious, those who are always funny, and those who are more religious than God. I have always warmed to people whose lives are a blend of seriousness and kindly humour. Such was Benjamin Franklin, the distinguished American. As well as being an eminent statesman, diplomat and scientist, the inventor of the lightning conductor and bifocal spectacles, he had a lively sense of humour. He was so renowned for delivering comic insights into serious discussions and debates, that some of his biographers believe that the reason Thomas Jefferson, rather than Franklin was asked to write the final draft of the Declaration of Independence was that some of the Founding Fathers suspected that Franklin might include a touch of humour in this extremely serious document!

❋

I remember doing what, alas, I do quite often, I dialled a wrong number. Embarrassed, I initiated the usual response: 'Oh, I am so sorry... ' But in mid-sentence I was interrupted. The voice was warm. It assured me that my error caused no real problem. I was left with the clear impression that I was on the receiving end of a full measure of goodwill that was just waiting for an opportunity to be poured out on someone. I came off the phone marvelling that my mistake had resulted in receiving such a blessing.

❋

Shortly after the *Titanic* sank in 1912, an American newspaper put two drawings side by side. One showed the great liner being smashed by the iceberg, and many people drowning in the cruel sea. Underneath were the words, 'The Weakness of Man, the Supremacy of Nature'. But the second picture showed a man stepping back in order to give a mother and child the last place in the lifeboat. Below this picture was the caption: 'The Supremacy of Man, the Weakness of Nature'. In these two drawings the artist managed to sum up one of the essential truths about human nature — that the secret of our real worth and supremacy lies in our ability to care and share, to make sacrifices for a greater good.